ST. BENEDICT: MONK, MYSTIC, EXORCIST

CATHOLIC SHOP

Catholic
Shop
.com

PROLOGUS

I n the verdant heart of Italy there once stood a towering temple dedicated to Apollo, its bronze idols glinting in the sun as worshippers came to sacrifice wolves, hawks, and other animals with the hope of pleasing their gods.

In the years after the fall of the Roman Empire, however, the temple became little more than a ruin, its stone columns and altar long-since stripped of anything valuable.

And so, in the 6th Century, when St. Benedict and his monks took on the task of converting the temple into a Christian chapel, it wasn't long before the entire structure lay in ruins, dismantled stone by stone.

One day as they worked, the monks stumbled upon a forgotten relic—a bronze idol hidden in the rubble of the temple.

Intrigued yet apprehensive, they brought the idol to the monastery kitchen, setting it beside the roaring hearth, intending to discard it later.

No sooner had they retreated from the room, however, the idol suddenly erupted into flames. The fire roared and danced, threatening to consume everything in its wake, striking fear in the monks. The monastery kitchen and adjacent rooms seemed doomed.

Summoned amidst the chaos, St. Benedict arrived. The sight of roaring flames and smoke billowing high did nothing to shake his serene demeanor. He recognized this not as a natural fire but as a supernatural manifestation. The idol, he insisted, was a vestige of pagan worship, and a vessel for demonic power.

Determined to vanquish the evil that threatened the monastery, Benedict fell to his knees, his voice steady despite the tumult around him. His prayer echoed through the room, rising above the crackling fire, his faith unwavering.

With each uttered word, the flames receded, gradually losing their intensity until Benedict whispered a final prayer and they disappeared as swiftly as they had ignited.

The demon, however, was unwilling to be bested so easily. He turned his wrath towards the construction of the monastery's new chapel.

The devil himself appeared to Benedict, smirking with malevolent glee as he threatened to bury the monks beneath the chapel they were building.

Benedict yelled out an urgent warning to his working monks, but it was too late. A once sturdy wall had collapsed, trapping one of the monks under a pile of rubble. Moments later, the other monks watched in horror as their brother was unearthed, lifeless.

Yet Benedict, though stricken with grief, remained composed.

In the chilling silence, he knelt beside the crushed body, his voice once again lifting in fervent prayer. His plea to the heavens was charged with desperation, his faith put to the ultimate test. He begged for divine intervention, for the restoration of his disciple's life.

The monks and onlookers held their breath, beholding Benedict's conviction as time seemed to stretch endlessly. Suddenly, the dead monk stirred. A collective gasp echoed through the ruins as the once lifeless form coughed, blinked, and sat up, alive and unharmed.

In that moment, the terrifying spectacle of the demonic fire and the miraculous resurrection of the monk were forever etched into history, fortifying St. Benedict's reputation as a man of miracles, a powerful exorcist, and a beloved spiritual guide.

Benedict's road to holiness had, in fact, begun many years before, when he gave up a life of privilege to commune with God in the isolation of a cold, dark cave.

Meet Benedict of Nursia, reader of souls, vanquisher of evil spirits, born a twin amidst the ruins of the Roman empire.

This is Benedict—mystic, monk, prophet, seer, and exorcist—an enigmatic man whose longing for the peace of God inspired him to shun the world and become a subterranean hermit, and a saint who now serves as an example for every Christian seeking to navigate the spiritual wilderness of the world.

PRAEFATIO

The Church is steeped in tradition and history, richly adorned by the narratives of countless men and women who, in their lives, strived to live out Christ's teachings. These saints are spiritual giants, their stories offering inspiration and guidance for followers of the faith.

One such towering figure is **Saint St. Benedict of Nursia.**

In the history of Christendom, few saints have imprinted the world as significantly as Benedict, the patriarch of Western monasticism and the author of a monastic rule that has endured for over fifteen centuries.

This book sets out to explore the remarkable life of Benedict, highlighting not only his exemplary life of faith and holiness but also the many miracles and prophecies that punctuated his journey on earth.

Benedict's life is one marked by exceptional moments that defy human understanding—moments that clearly attest to the divine hand operating in his life.

From his survival of two poisoning attempts, the miraculous mending of a broken sieve, to his prophetic visions of the future of his monastery, Benedict's life is a testament to the power of God manifested in those who dedicate themselves entirely to His service.

But the miraculous elements of Benedict's story do not exist in isolation—they are inextricably tied to his profound faith and unwavering devotion.

As we explore these miraculous incidents, we also delve into the depths of his spiritual insight, his relentless pursuit of God, his remarkable capacity to discern and resist temptation, and many of the times he went to battle against forces of evil and won.

Benedict's impact, however, reverberates far beyond the confines of his time. His Rule continues to guide monastic life, shaping the spirituality and daily rhythm of countless communities around the world.

Its principles, founded on moderation, community, and a balance of prayer and work, have also found resonance outside monastic circles, providing wisdom and direction to laypeople in their quest for spiritual growth.

Yet, Benedict's legacy is not confined to his Rule or to his influence on monasticism. He is a towering figure in the Church for his role as a protector against evil and temptation—a role vividly symbolized in the St. Benedict Medal, a powerful sacramental often invoked in spiritual warfare.

His life is a beacon of light in a world often besieged by spiritual darkness, reminding us of the power of faith, the strength of divine protection, and the promise of God's triumphant grace.

In the vast spiritual battlefield of human existence, Saint St. Benedict of Nursia stands as a stalwart soldier, a beacon of faith and courage against the forces of darkness.

As the pages of his life unfold, we see Benedict not just as the founder of Western Monasticism and the author of the Rule that guides countless souls towards a godly path, but also as a formidable exorcist, a sentinel of right-eousness facing down the harbingers of evil.

His life was punctuated by continual encounters with demonic forces, yet each confrontation highlighted Benedict's unwavering faith and resilience. He emerged from these spiritual skirmishes not only unscathed but triumphantly victorious, casting out evil spirits, undoing their malevolent workings, and restoring spiritual peace to the afflicted.

From his battles against disruptive spirits within his own community to his dramatic confrontations with diabolical possession, his life bears testament to the spiritual warfare that he waged.

As we delve into his life, we find Benedict casting his radiant shield of faith in the shadowy valleys of evil, his prayers serving as powerful incantations to exorcise malevolent entities.

Thus, Saint Benedict's legacy is etched not just in his holy rule, but also in his heroic battles against the darkness which continue to this day, truly marking him as an exorcist for the ages.

This book is an invitation to journey through the extraordinary life of Benedict, to glean from his wisdom, be inspired by his faith, and witness the wondrous workings of the divine in his life.

As we embark on this exploration, may we discover fresh insights and inspirations for our own spiritual journeys and deepen our understanding of this beloved saint's enduring relevance and protection in our contemporary world

PART I

BENEDICTUS

Let us open our eyes to the light that comes from God, and our ears to the voice from heaven...

- Benedict

1

FROM RICHES TO RAGS

Born alongside his twin sister, Scholastic, in the small Italian town of Nursia, Benedict came of age during a time of significant upheaval. The year was 480 AD, and the Western Roman Empire had recently collapsed, giving rise to an era of political and social chaos.

His early years were marked by significant events and experiences that not only indicated his future spirituality but also provided a fertile ground for his development as a Christian ascetic.

Amid this tumult, Benedict's affluent parents managed to send him to Rome for studies. However, disappointed by the city's moral decadence, he withdrew from worldly life and retreated to the solitude of a cave in Subiaco.

For three years, Benedict led a life of seclusion and prayer in Subiaco. His holy reputation gradually attracted many followers, prompting him to establish a dozen small monasteries in the vicinity. Unfortunately, Benedict faced opposition, envy, and even attempts on his life. He eventually decided to leave Subiaco, along with a group of disciples, and journeyed to Monte Cassino.

At Monte Cassino, situated halfway between Rome and Naples, Benedict built his crowning achievement: a large monastery intended to be a beacon of Christian life. Here, he wrote the 'Rule of St. Benedict,' a set of precepts for monks living communally under the authority of an abbot. The Rule, encapsulated in the maxim "Ora et Labora" (Pray and Work), provided a balance between spiritual and manual work, emphasizing humility, obedience, and above all, the love of Christ and neighbor.

Benedict was also known for his extraordinary spiritual gifts. His gift of prophecy was attested to in numerous accounts, from foreseeing the destruction of his own monastery in Monte Cassino to predicting the day of his death.

His profound visions, another one of his spiritual gifts, were not only a source of personal revelation but also provided guidance and wisdom to his followers. They were at times practical, revealing the presence of hidden food during times of scarcity, and at times they were deeply mystical, like his renowned vision of the world in a single ray of sunlight, symbolizing the interconnectedness of all creation.

Healing, too, was a part of his miraculous gifts. He was said to have healed numerous people, from monks in his own community to the Roman patrician, Servandus. And, on multiple occasions, he reportedly drove out evil spirits, enhancing his reputation as a spiritual warrior against evil forces. His ability to survive attempts on his life through divine intervention, including being poisoned twice, further testify to the supernatural protection that enveloped him.

Benedict passed away on March 21, 547 AD, having accurately foreseen and predicted the circumstances and exact date, but his legacy lived on in an extraordinary way.

The 'Rule of St. Benedict' became the foundational text for monastic life in the West. Monasteries following his Rule proliferated across Europe, preserving literacy and learning during the Middle Ages when much of the continent was plunged into darkness.

2

NURSIA

In the shadow of the Sibillini Mountains, nestled in the verdant heart of Italy, lies the ancient town of Nursia, the birthplace of Benedict. Born into a noble family around the year 480, Benedict and his twin sister Scholastica were destined to have profound impacts on the Christian world.

Nursia, in the early 5th century, was a rural sanctuary far removed from the bustling metropolises of the Roman Empire. Framed by mountains and painted with the colors of nature, it provided a serene backdrop to Benedict's early life. The cultural influence of ancient Rome would have been significant, given that the fall of the Western Roman Empire had only occurred a few decades prior.

Today, Norcia—located in the same region of Italy as Assisi, birthplace of St. Francis—is a popular destination for religious pilgrims, history enthusiasts, and food lovers alike. It is renowned for its gastronomy, particularly truffles, ham, and other pork products, which are celebrated in annual festivals. The town is home to a variety of specialty food shops, called "Norcineria," that sell these regional delicacies.

The town's historical center, which was severely damaged by an earthquake in 2016, is still undergoing restoration but continues to draw visitors. The Basilica of Benedict, the saint's birthplace, is one of the main attractions, although it was also affected by the earthquake.

Despite its small size, Norcia is still home to a monastic community of Benedictine monks who follow the Rule of St. Benedict. They serve the local community and visitors through their prayers, hospitality, and production of monastic goods such as beer and liturgical vestments.

In Benedict's time, Nursia would have been a modest Roman town located on the Via Salaria, an important salt route. Living in the period of transition from the classical Roman world to the Middle Ages, young Benedict would have experienced a society in flux.

Benedict was born into a well-to-do, noble Roman family, indicating a background of comfort and refinement. The family's socio-economic status likely afforded Benedict the literacy and learning that enabled him to study scripture and spiritual writings, and to convey his thoughts in written form, while the post-empire environment likely contributed to his eventual establishment of the monastic life that would shape Western Christianity in the centuries to follow.

Benedict's early education likely began at home under the guidance of a tutor, a common practice among Roman nobility. His privileged birth meant that his early education would have been grounded in the Roman classics, equipping him with the knowledge and skills that he would later incorporate into his Rule.

As a child in Nursia, he would have learned the basics of reading and writing, mathematics, and perhaps even some elementary teachings of philosophy and ethics. As he advanced, the curriculum would have broadened to include more complex subjects such as rhetoric, music, astronomy, and the study of classic Greek and Roman texts.

Life in Nursia would have revolved around agriculture, trade, and local Roman governance structures. The rhythm of seasons, the tilling of the earth, the simplicity and hardiness of rural life, all wove a tapestry of humility and grounding, imparting lessons of patience, resilience, and the dignity of manual labor.

It was within the nurturing confines of this humble town that Benedict's spiritual inclination likely took root. Christianity was increasingly influential during this time, and Nursia, like many towns, had its community of believers. The teachings of Christ, as conveyed by local clergy and devout laity, may well have found a receptive audience in young Benedict.

Family life, too, would have played an integral role in his spiritual formation. Being Roman nobles, his parents would have been educated and, likely, deeply religious. As such, they would have felt a commitment to provide their children with a Christian upbringing. The values of hospitality, charity, integrity, and faith were likely instilled from an early age, shaping Benedict's moral compass.

This upbringing would have included learning the scriptures, attending the Eucharistic celebration, and living in the community of the faithful. This early immersion in Christian faith and life likely had a significant impact on his spiritual formation, planting the seeds of his later decision to dedicate his life to God.

Nursia, during Benedict's lifetime, would have had the characteristics of a typical Roman town, complete with a forum, baths, and temples turned into Christian churches after the Edict of Milan in 313 AD made Christianity legal.

The landscape surrounding the town would have been much the same as it is today.

The beauty and solitude of the Umbrian landscape could have naturally drawn his mind to contemplation, paving the way for his later monastic orientation. Benedict seemed to have been touched by a longing for solitude and communion with God from an early age. Nursia, with its rugged landscape, could have served as the perfect canvas upon which the first strokes of this yearning were painted. The mountains, with their silent strength, echoed the call to solitude. The vast sky overhead, dotted with stars, whispered of the divine mystery. The quiet rustling of the forest sang a hymn to the Creator. Nature, in its silent eloquence, invited Benedict into a deep, intimate dialogue with God.

It is not implausible to think that his childhood in Nursia, away from the bustling urban life of Rome, played a significant role in shaping his spirituality.

His parents, wishing to secure for their son the best education, sent him to Rome for his higher studies. Although this was a common practice for families of their status, it may have been this early exposure to secular education that later influenced Benedict's decision to abandon it in favor of a life of solitude and prayer.

3

ROME TO ROAM

Around the dawn of the 5th century, Rome was a city of contrasts. Once the radiant capital of a world-spanning empire, it was now a labyrinth of glory and decay, resplendent grandeur sitting shoulder to shoulder with the crumbling echoes of a bygone era.

Into this city, the cradle of civilization, teeming with humanity and pulsating with the hum of urban life, entered young St. Benedict of Nursia, ready to pursue higher studies

A city of grandeur and complexity, Rome was the epicenter of cultural, political, and educational pursuits in the fifth century. Benedict's journey to Rome, therefore, marked a significant transition from the quiet, rural life in Nursia to the heart of the empire. With Rome's vast libraries, revered teachers, and intellectual fervor, it promised unparalleled opportunities for a young man seeking higher education.

For a young man from a small town, Rome would have been an assault on the senses, its bustling streets, grand public buildings, forums, temples, theaters, and baths a testament to its grandeur. However, beneath this vibrant exterior, the city was experiencing the aftershocks of the fall of the Western Roman Empire, with societal structures under strain and moral fabric fraying at the edges.

Benedict, a keen observer, noticed the moral decay of the city. The classrooms where he sought knowledge were filled with raucous laughter, rampant hedonism, and distractions of worldly pleasures. Rome, in its degradation, was a city where vice was lauded, and virtue became the casualty.

Benedict began his formal studies in law and literature. His advanced studies in Rome would have been more specialized than his early education in Nursia. As part of his legal training, he would have studied the works of Cicero, Ulpian, and other great Roman legal minds, along with in-depth studies of the Justinian Code, an important compilation of Roman law.

Studying literature in Rome, Benedict would have been introduced to the rich tapestry of Latin literature, diving deep into the works of Vergil, Ovid, and Horace, who once wrote, *"Wisdom is not wisdom when it is derived from books alone."*

Benedict might have also read Greek classics in translation, engaging with the poetic epics of Homer, the dialogues of Plato, and the historical accounts of Herodotus and Thucydides. These works, teeming with tales of heroism, morality, love, and intrigue, would have furthered his understanding of human nature, influenced his involvement in society, and filtered the lens through which he experienced life in Rome.

Despite the city's intellectual allure, Rome's moral landscape proved to be a stark contrast. The city, at the zenith of its influence, was rife with corruption and decadence. The moral laxity that permeated the society deeply disturbed

Benedict, who was striving to live a life of Christian virtue. The licentious lifestyle of his fellow students, the rampant corruption, and the disregard for moral integrity deeply disturbed Benedict. In this swirling whirlpool of decadence, the seeds of solitude began to sprout in his heart.

Benedict's education in Rome, thus, was a period of intellectual growth and moral disillusionment. His experiences there fueled his increasing desire to break away from the secular world and devote himself to spiritual pursuits. The young scholar from Nursia found himself at a crossroads, torn between the intellectual richness of Rome and the spiritual poverty he perceived in its worldly pursuits. Rome, with its cacophony and chaos, its grandeur and decay, became the crucible that shaped Benedict's early spiritual life, propelling him towards his destiny.

In Rome, it's likely that Benedict also encountered Christianity in its manifold expressions. Rome was, after all, a melting pot of cultures and religions, and Christianity was already exerting its influence across societal strata. Perhaps he heard the Gospel message or observed the faith-filled lives of the humble followers of Christ, their actions speaking louder than the shouts of the rowdy crowds. These encounters might have stoked the embers of spirituality within him, fanning them into a flame that sought communion with the divine, away from the distractions of city life.

And so, the stage was set for a transformation. He yearned for an escape from the moral maelstrom that the once glorious city had become, yearned to retreat into silence where the still, small voice of God could be heard. The culmination of Benedict's experiences in Rome, his exposure to its grandeur and its grim realities, would soon lead him to abandon his life there and retreat into solitude, forever changing the course of Christianity.

Thus, a young scholar, disillusioned by the ways of men, embarked on a journey both spiritual and physical— a wandering pilgrim-explorer who would soon morph into a beacon of spiritual light, guiding countless souls across centuries towards God.

PART II

SANCTUS

*Listen carefully, my son, to the master's instructions, and
attend to them with the ear of your heart.*

- Benedict

4

THE CAVE

Benedict's time in Subiaco was marked by spiritual development and the establishment of monastic communities, but it was also a period fraught with challenge and conflict.

After leaving the simple life he had known in Nursia to study in Rome, the socio-political situation of the time and the instability left over after the fall of the Western Roman Empire is likely to have played a pivotal role in Benedict's decision to turn his eye from higher education to spiritual development.

Benedict was the progeny of Roman nobility, a lineage that promised him a life of comfort and prestige. But, during his time in Rome, the longing for spiritual fulfillment that began to stir in him led him to a decision that would alter the course of his life.

Witnessing the societal turmoil during his student life in Rome undoubtedly had some influence on Benedict's decision to withdraw from worldly life and seek God in solitude and prayer. Perhaps some of Benedict's classical and philosophical studies also served as inspiration, such as the ancient Roman poet Vergil, who once wrote *"The hour is ripe, and yonder lies the way."*

Shunning the opulence and wealth of his father's house, Benedict departed from Rome accompanied by a loyal servant and driven by a fervent aspiration to serve God as a hermit.

In the wake of his escape from the debauchery of Rome, Benedict and his servant journeyed through the hills and valleys of Italy, on a path guided not by worldly desire, but by a fervent longing for God. They had no final destination for their journey and eventually found themselves in the rugged Sabine Mountains, some thirty miles away from the bustling metropolis of Rome.

"A man who is a monk not only in name, but also in deed, ought to be one who is dead to all the affairs of this world."
 - The Rule of St. Benedict, Chapter 4

Barely twenty years old, Benedict and his servant sought refuge in a village named Enfide, nestled in the mountains, a mere thirty miles away from the turmoil of Rome. Enfide, steeped in natural beauty, was a far cry from the busy streets and decadent lifestyle of the city. The simple and rustic life of the villagers offered a contrasting backdrop to the sophisticated urban world that Benedict had known. His stay was short-lived, but not before a miraculous event that revealed the hand of God working through him.

In a remarkable incident, Benedict's servant accidentally broke an earthenware sieve that belonged to a neighbor. Stricken with distress at the loss of a treasured item, the servant was comforted by Benedict, who took the fragments of the broken sieve, knelt down, prayed.

To the amazement of onlookers, the sieve was made whole again. News of the miracle quickly spread among the villagers, which, to Benedict's discomfort, brought undue attention and adulation. To avoid the ensuing praise and gossip amongst the villagers, and in an effort to maintain his humility, he and his servant sought solitude once more, journeying further into the hills and finally to the wilderness of Subiaco, a place that seemed imbued with divine tranquility.

Here, Benedict encountered an older man named Romanus, and shared with him his profound desire to embrace the monastic life. Romanus lived as a monk in a hilltop community located in the region. Unbeknownst to Benedict, Romanus would play a pivotal role in shaping his monastic life, and the solitude he had been yearning for was about to take form in an isolated cave that would be his home for the next three years.

Upon meeting him, Romanus was instantly struck by the young man's fervor and commitment to leading a hermit's life, and he decided to guide and support him. To encourage Benedict's devotion, Romanus offered him shelter in a cave located in the wilderness below his community and provided him with his own habit, one made of animal skins.

And so, in the solitude of the wilderness, hidden away from the world in a cave, shunning the traps and temptations of the world he had known, Benedict began living as a hermit. He would live there for three years, relying on the providence of God, often delivered through Romanus, and developing a deeper sense of communion with the Divine.

St. Gregory the Great in his "Dialogues" describes Romanus as a monk of exemplary virtue. His first interaction with Benedict is indeed a testament to his compassion and understanding. It is said that Romanus, whose community was perched above Benedict's cave, would secretly lower with a long piece of rope with a bell attached to alert Benedict to its arrival.

This way, Romanus ensured that the young hermit could focus on prayer and contemplation without worrying about his physical needs. In many ways, without the help of Romanus, Benedict's newfound life of solitary prayer and contemplation might not have resulted in the profound spiritual movement it would become.

As for miracles associated with Romanus, one of the most notable occurred around the issue of the daily bread. The abbot of Romanus' community became suspicious of his daily absence at the time he took the bread to Benedict. To satisfy his curiosity, he followed Romanus and found out about his support of the young hermit.

The abbot, either out of jealousy or misunderstanding, decided to punish Romanus. However, when he tried to whip him, his arm became paralyzed and stayed in the air. It was only after he pleaded for Romanus' forgiveness that his arm was restored. This miracle not only saved Romanus from an unjust punishment but also reinforced the sanctity of his mission to support Benedict.

Romanus' life underscores the importance of spiritual fraternity and guidance. His kindness and support of Benedict during his early years of spiritual formation played a vital role in the making of a saint who would go on to impact the Christian world significantly. Though his name is often overshadowed by the greatness of Benedict, Romanus' life serves as a testament to the beauty of humble, sacrificial service

In a poignant note on Romanus' passing, St. Gregory the Great tells us that Benedict was informed of his death by a vision. As he was praying in his cave, he saw the soul of

Romanus ascend to heaven. It was a fitting end for the humble monk who, in serving another, had himself soared to the heights of sanctity.

5

COMMUNITY

Near the winding course of the Aniene River, amidst the rugged, wild hills of the Italian landscape, the young Benedict had found his sanctuary in the natural fortress of a rocky cave near Subiaco.

Here, nestled amidst the verdant landscape and hidden beneath an overhanging cliff, lay the remnants of one of Roman Emperor Nero's opulent villas – an ironic parallel between the hedonistic life of the decadent emperor and the ascetic existence that Benedict had chosen. In Benedict's time, Subiaco was a quiet, rural area. Its name comes from the artificial lake ('Sublaqueum') below which it was situated, created by Nero for his villa.

The solitude of the cave, far from being a desolate experience, became a fertile ground for Benedict's spiritual growth. His was a solitude that reverberated with the echoes of contemplation, prayer, and a relentless quest for divine union. In this hermitage, where the boundaries between the divine and the human seemed to blur, Benedict not only cultivated his relationship with God but also developed the framework of what would later become his Rule.

Within this quiet solitude, Benedict's presence did not go unnoticed. Shepherds tending their flocks in the nearby fields discovered the holy man. Their initial curiosity soon transformed into a profound reverence for the hermit, who, despite his solitude, exuded a divine serenity and wisdom. Over time, these humble shepherds became his disciples in spirit, learning from Benedict the teachings of the Gospel, imbibing his way of prayer and asceticism, and witnessing his miracles and prophecies.

Later, as Benedict's reputation spread, these shepherds played an integral role in attracting more followers. The friendships forged in those early years at Subiaco laid the cornerstone for what was to become one of the most influential monastic communities of the Christian world.

In this way, the secluded cave near Nero's crumbling villa became a beacon of spiritual illumination, the shepherds the first disciples of a man destined to shape the monastic tradition, and Benedict, the humble hermit, became a spiritual father to many.

Romanus was not always able to bring food for Benedict, perhaps due to his abbot's watchful eye. It was during one such time, however, that Benedict witnessed another example of the beauty of divine providence, the solidarity among those who seek to live in obedience to God's will, and the deep spiritual communion that links all members of the Body of Christ.

During one Holy Saturday, the day before Easter Sunday, Benedict was alone in his cave with no food. Meanwhile, in a divine act of providence, a priest in a nearby town was preparing a special meal to celebrate Easter. While sitting at his table, the priest heard a voice saying,

"You are feasting luxuriously while my servant Benedict is afflicted with hunger."

Recognizing this as a divine command, the priest immediately set out in search of Benedict. Despite the remoteness of the location and the fact that he didn't know where Benedict was staying, the priest was miraculously led to the cave.

There, he shared his Easter meal with Benedict, who was grateful for the timely provision. They spent time in prayer and spiritual conversation before the priest left, leaving Benedict to continue his hermitage. This event serves as an early indicator of Benedict's sanctity and his deep communion with God, as well as a powerful testament to trust in divine providence.

It was also in this period, however, that Benedict's reputation for sanctity became a threat to the tranquility he had come to embrace. As news of a hermit who lived on the generosity of others continued to spread, more and more people began to seek him out, bringing offerings of food. Benedict's quest for solitude became a beacon, drawing followers towards a life of piety and spiritual pursuit, and Benedict could not turn them away.

The Subiaco of today is located within the Metropolitan City of Rome, in the region of Lazio, central Italy. It's known as a beautiful town that attracts both religious pilgrims and tourists. Perched on a hillside, the town offers stunning views of the Aniene River Valley below.

The town is characterized by winding streets, restored ancient houses, beautiful squares, and historical monuments. The local economy thrives on tourism, agriculture, and traditional local crafts. And, just as in Benedict's Day when his reputation began to spread, Subiaco's biggest draw is its monastic complex: the Monastery of St. Scholastica and the Sacro Speco (Holy Cave), which houses the Monastery of Benedict.

Sacro Speco continues to draw pilgrims who go there to soak in its deep spiritual significance, see the place where Benedict lived as a hermit, and contemplate in the same solitude that this great saint once sought. Despite the passing of the centuries, the cave still retains the powerful aura of sanctity associated with the life of Benedict.

Many are surprised, however, to see that the cave in which Benedict lived is quite small, while others note that its small size makes it all the more fitting for a hermit seeking solitude. There's now an altar in the cave, and above it, a fresco depicts Benedict's time as a hermit, his temptation by the devil, and his victory over temptation.

In the 5th-century, as Benedict's fame grew, so did the number of his disciples, prompting him to establish twelve small monasteries in the vicinity, each housing twelve monks and a superior. Benedict himself oversaw these monasteries, nurturing them with his spiritual wisdom.

His ascetic lifestyle and the monastic discipline he promoted, however, were not welcomed by all.

6

THE POISON CUP

The saga of Benedict's spiritual journey is not a linear progression of tranquil contemplation and uninterrupted piety. His sojourn in Vicovaro, a small town near Tivoli, offers a striking testament to his trials and triumphs amidst adversity and temptation.

Benedict's survival of attempted poisoning is one of the most well-known stories about his life, and it comes from St. Gregory the Great's *Dialogues*, a primary source of information about Benedict.

Upon the request of a local community, Benedict had agreed to leave Subiaco and become the abbot of a monastery in Vicovaro. The monks, dissatisfied with their previous abbot's stern rule, had hoped for a more lenient leadership under Benedict. However, they soon found that Benedict, guided by his deep-rooted faith and his commitment to spiritual discipline, was not inclined to laxity.

Benedict's strict adherence to the monastic rules and his ascetic way of life did not sit well with the other monks. The austerity and discipline he advocated as the prior of the community were viewed as excessively harsh by the monks who had a more relaxed interpretation of monastic living. Struggling with his rigorous standards, the monks grew resentful.

In an extreme demonstration of their discontent, and feeling threatened by the changes he was instigating, they plotted to poison their holy leader to rid themselves of his leadership. One day, they laced his drink with poison and served it to him.

Divine providence, however, had other plans.

When presented with the tainted drink, as was his custom, Benedict performed the sign of the cross over the cup before he drank from it. As he made the sign of the cross, however, the cup that held the poisoned drink shattered, spilling its contents. This miraculous event is interpreted as divine intervention to save Benedict's life.

Benedict's response to this treachery was marked by a serene acceptance of human failings, a testament to his extraordinary spiritual maturity. Realizing that the community did not share his commitment to strict monastic observance, he chose not to punish the monks but to leave Vicovaro, returning to the cavernous solitude he had come to embrace.

The experience at Vicovaro also likely influenced his later approach to monastic life, leading him to establish his own monasteries where the rigors of monastic discipline could be fully observed. His time in Vicovaro, despite its short duration, is a testament to Benedict's unwavering commitment to his spiritual ideals.

The event is often depicted in artwork related to Benedict, emphasizing the miraculous protection granted to him. It is also commemorated in the design of the St. Benedict Medal, which includes the image of the cup and a raven, which is associated with another poisoning attempt that Benedict survived.

7

THE POISON BREAD

The second attempt on Benedict's life through poisoning is another memorable incident from his life. This event, like the first, is recorded in St. Gregory the Great's "Dialogues".

After leaving Vicovaro, Benedict returned to Subiaco and established a series of monasteries. His reputation for holiness and wisdom attracted many, but it also aroused the envy and malice of a local priest named Florentius.

Florentius became envious of Benedict due to the growing reputation of the young monastic leader. As Benedict attracted more and more followers, Florentius perceived him as a threat to his own prestige and influence. This envy fueled a bitter conflict, which involved several attempts by Florentius to harm or discredit Benedict.

In the first instance, Florentius tried to tarnish Benedict's reputation by sending seven promiscuous women into the monastery to distract the monks and lead them into sin. However, upon seeing them, Benedict immediately realized the danger and fled the monastery with a few monks, going to live in the mountains near Subiaco.

Unable to bear Benedict's growing influence, Florentius resolved to kill him. He sent to Benedict a loaf of bread laced with poison. But Benedict, who had the gift of discernment, seemed to know that the bread was poisoned; he commanded a raven, which had been coming to him daily for a piece of bread, to take the poisoned loaf and dispose of it where no one could find it. The raven complied, and when it returned, Benedict gave the bird his blessing.

The story of the raven and the poisoned bread is often depicted in art about Benedict, emphasizing the saint's deep connection with creation and his divine protection. The incident is also symbolized on the St. Benedict Medal, with the raven and the poisoned loaf depicted alongside the shattered cup from the first poisoning attempt.

Lastly, in his blind envy and rage, Florentius plotted to destroy the monastic buildings at Subiaco by collapsing them. However, before the plan could be carried out, the building in which Florentius himself was standing collapsed, killing him instantly. Benedict, upon hearing the news, was deeply sorrowful for the tragic end of Florentius.

The conflict with Florentius is significant as it highlights the opposition Benedict faced due to his growing influence and the establishment of his monastic communities. Moreover, the way Benedict handled these situations – with patience, wisdom, and compassion – offers insight into his character and holiness.

8

BODY AND BLOOD

The poison cup and poison bread that were given to Benedict in an attempt to cause his death present an interesting antithesis to the Eucharistic celebration and the Last Supper, where Jesus shares a cup of wine and bread, symbolizing his blood and body, with his disciples.

A similar connection is found in John 6:35:

Jesus said to them, "I am the bread of life; whoever comes to me will never hunger, and whoever believes in me will never thirst."

The Eucharist, or the Last Supper, which was certainly foreshadowed throughout the Bible, is a central event in Christianity, symbolizing Jesus' sacrifice for the salvation of humanity. The bread represents Jesus' body, given for mankind, and the wine represents His blood, shed for the remission of sins. This act invites the faithful to partake in divine life.

Contrarily, the incidents involving poison in the life of Benedict, namely the poison cup and poison bread episodes, subvert this sacred symbolism. Instead of the

Bread of Life, Benedict was given a cup of poison and bread of death by his enemies.

The intended effect of the poison, of course, is not to nourish or give life, but to harm or take life away. Instead of unity and covenant, the poison symbolizes treachery and hostility. However, in both cases, there is a miraculous element.

In the Eucharistic celebration, the bread and wine miraculously become the body and blood of Christ through transubstantiation. In the episodes of Benedict, the intended harm of the poison is miraculously neutralized – the poison cup shatters when Benedict blesses it, and a raven carries away the poison bread on Benedict's command.

Ultimately, while the poison cup and poison bread served as an antithesis to the Eucharistic symbols of the chalice of wine and bread of life, they also bear testament to the divine protection and intervention in preserving the life of a saint, showcasing the triumph of divine providence over human malice.

There are numerous other ways in which the most notable events in Benedict's life seem to mirror the life of Jesus.

Both men were founders. Jesus, of course, was the founder of Christianity, while Benedict is often called the founder of Western monasticism. Both established a 'way of life' that have millions of followers worldwide.

Both Jesus and Benedict faced temptations. Jesus was tempted by Satan in the desert, while Benedict faced temptation from the devil during his time as a hermit in the wilderness. Both overcame these challenges, setting examples of spiritual fortitude.

Jesus had his disciples, who spread His teachings after His ascension. Similarly, Benedict attracted many followers, who established monasteries across Europe based on his Rule, thereby preserving and promoting Christian culture during the Middle Ages and beyond.

The legacies of both Jesus and Benedict continue to be influential. The teachings of Jesus form the core of Christian faith, while the Rule of St. Benedict still guides monastic life and offers wisdom to lay people as well.

Despite the similarities, however, they hold very different places within the faith. Benedict is venerated as a holy man and a guide to monastic and Christian life, while Jesus, the Son of God and the Savior of humanity, was very reason behind Benedict's choice to live a life of virtue and prayer in the first place.

The two instances of attempted poisoning, and Benedict's miraculous survival, greatly contributed to his reputation as a holy man protected by God. Benedict's life was fraught with tribulation and persecution, and the conflict between Benedict and men who wished to kill him is one of the ways in which Benedict became associated with protection from evil.

Thankfully, Benedict's leadership and the communal strength of the monastic brotherhood resisted these destructive efforts. But the repeated attacks and escalating envy from opponents compelled Benedict to leave Subiaco. So, accompanied by a group of his loyal monks, he moved south to establish the famous monastery of Monte Cassino, marking the end of his time in Subiaco.

Despite the opposition he faced, the years in Subiaco were critical for Benedict. They shaped his spiritual vision, which would later be codified in his Rule, providing a foundation for the monastic tradition that continues

9

MONTE CASSINO

Benedict's arrival at Monte Cassino marked a turning point in his spiritual journey and in the history of monasticism in the Christian West. Located halfway between Rome and Naples, Monte Cassino was a prime location for Benedict's vision.

When he and his followers arrived around 529 AD, however, the place was far from being a holy site. A temple dedicated to Apollo stood there, surrounded by sacred groves worshipped by the local people. The temple was believed to be inhabited by a demon, which Benedict cast out.

Benedict carried on his work by smashing the pagan idol, cutting down the groves, and building a chapel dedicated to St. Martin of Tours and St. John the Baptist, thereby transforming the temple into a Christian church.

At Monte Cassino, Benedict established a monastic community which was to become the model for all future Benedictine monasteries. Here, he developed what we now know as the "Rule of St. Benedict," a practical guide for monastic life based on the principles of prayer, work, study, and communal living.

Unlike the twelve separate communities at Subiaco, Monte Cassino was one large community. Instead of having several superiors, there was now one abbot - Benedict himself. This centralized monastic life helped foster a sense of unity and community among the monks.

Monastic life at Monte Cassino was built around the cycle of "Ora et Labora," pray and work. The monks would gather seven times a day for liturgical prayers (the Divine Office) and would dedicate themselves to manual labor and sacred reading during the rest of the day.

Benedict's teachings attracted people from far and wide. Nobles, commoners, and even barbarian warlords sought his counsel. Despite his growing influence, Benedict remained a humble servant of God, exemplifying the virtues he preached - humility, obedience, and charity.

It was also during his time at Monte Cassino that Benedict performed many miracles, further cementing his reputation as a holy man. One of the most well-known miracles is the resurrection of a young monk who had died in a construction accident.

Despite the many achievements of his time at Monte Cassino, Benedict's life was not without challenges. He faced opposition from a local priest and was even accused of witchcraft. Yet, through it all, he remained steadfast, focused on his calling to live and promote a life of prayer and work dedicated to God.

Benedict lived at Monte Cassino for the rest of his life, continually inspiring and guiding his monastic brothers. His presence made Monte Cassino a beacon of spiritual and intellectual life amidst the turmoil of the early Middle Ages.

10

THE MONASTIC MODEL

Today, the Abbey of Monte Cassino stands as a testament to Benedict's enduring legacy. The monastery is located in the town of Cassino, in the province of Frosinone, central Italy, perched on a hilltop overlooking the town below. As a place of pilgrimage and prayer for people from all over the world, it is one of the most famous monasteries in the world.

The current abbey is a post-World War II reconstruction. During the Battle of Monte Cassino in 1944, the monastery was destroyed by Allied bombing but was rebuilt after the war, largely maintaining its original design. Today, it houses a museum and a library with a vast collection of manuscripts.

The abbey's grand Basilica, which is dedicated to St. Martin and Benedict, is filled with stunning mosaics, paintings, and chapels. It also contains the tombs of Benedict and his sister, St. Scholastica. The monastery is a spiritual and cultural center, hosting concerts, exhibitions, and conferences.

When Benedict arrived at Monte Cassino around 529

AD, the location was considerably different from what it is today. At that time, it was a hilltop site of a dilapidated fortress and a temple dedicated to Apollo, surrounded by a grove sacred to the local pagans.

Benedict chose this location to establish a monastery and to replace the pagan worship with Christian prayer. He destroyed the pagan temple and used the materials to build two chapels.

Benedict lived at Monte Cassino for the rest of his life, overseeing the spiritual and material needs of the monastery, while transforming Monte Cassino from a place of pagan worship into a beacon of Christian monasticism. It was also here that he wrote his famous "Rule."

The thriving monastic community attracted many visitors, leading to the establishment of a guest house and a hospital for the care of the sick and the poor. Benedict's choice to organize the monks into a single community marked the foundation of Benedictine monasticism and the shift from hermit-like monasticism to community life, which remains a model for religious life in the Western Church.

11

TWIN SAINTS

S t. Scholastica, the sister of St. Benedict of Nursia, is celebrated as a model of female sanctity and an instrumental figure in the early development of monasticism. Though information about her life is scarce, her deep spirituality and love for her brother have left a lasting imprint on the history of the Church.

Born in Nursia, Italy, around 480 AD, Scholastica was the twin sister of Benedict, who later became the founder of Western monasticism. The siblings came from a noble Roman family and were raised in a Christian household.

As twins, Scholastica and Benedict were particularly close, a relationship that would flourish into spiritual camaraderie. When Benedict left for Rome to receive formal education, Scholastica, too, was exposed to the spiritual teachings prevalent during that time. However, the immorality in Rome at the time was disturbing for both, and both siblings felt the call to religious life.

While Benedict left to pursue a hermit's life in Subiaco, it is believed that Scholastica also consecrated her life to

God at a young age, presumably remaining in her parental home and dedicating herself to God.

Like her brother, Scholastica felt a deep calling to monasticism. Around 530 AD, she established a community for women near Monte Cassino, the mountain-top monastery founded by her brother.

After Benedict established a monastery atop the mountain of Monte Cassino, located between Rome and Naples, Scholastica too felt a deep calling to monasticism. Inspired by her brother's commitment to the religious life, in or around the year 530 AD, she founded a convent for women approximately 5 miles from Monte Cassino.

Scholastica embraced the Rule of St. Benedict, becoming the first Benedictine nun. She mirrored her brother's mission, cultivating a community centered around prayer and work, and extending the influence of Benedictine spirituality to women.

Even though they led separate religious communities, the siblings maintained a close relationship. They met once a year in a farmhouse near the Monte Cassino monastery, spending the day in prayer and spiritual conversation.

The most famous story about Scholastica, as told by Pope St. Gregory the Great in his "Dialogues," occurred during their last meeting. Sensing that her death was near, Scholastica wished to extend their conversation into the night. However, Benedict was reluctant to break his own rule, which required him to spend the night in his monastery.

In response, Scholastica prayed fervently, and a severe thunderstorm broke out, making it impossible for Benedict to leave. Moved by this, Benedict exclaimed, *"God forgive you, sister. What have you done?"*

Scholastica simply replied, *"I asked a favor of you, and you refused. I asked it of God, and He granted it."*

Three days after this meeting, in 543 AD, Scholastica passed away. In a dream, Benedict saw her soul leaving her body and ascending to heaven in the form of a dove, signifying her purity and freedom.

Benedict had her body brought to Monte Cassino, where he laid it to rest in the tomb he had prepared for himself. When Benedict died around 547, he was buried alongside his sister, solidifying their spiritual bond even in death.

Scholastica's legacy is primarily known through the lens of her relationship with her brother. Her life, though more obscure than Benedict's, stands as a testament to the place of women in the early Church's monastic tradition. She was a leader in her own right, heading a community of religious women and deeply influencing her brother.

Her insistence on the importance of spiritual communion, as seen in the story of their final meeting, had a profound effect on Benedict. The incident revealed not only the depth of their sibling love but also their mutual respect and spiritual connection.

Recognized as a saint by the tradition of the Church, Scholastica's feast day is celebrated on February 10. She is the patron saint of nuns, convulsive children, and is invoked against storms and rain.

The relationship between St. Scholastica and Benedict continues to inspire the faithful, reminding us of the beauty of spiritual kinship, the importance of persistent prayer, and the influential role of women in the Church's history. The bond between these holy siblings illustrates that our journey towards God does not occur in isolation, but in communion with our fellow believers.

St. Scholastica, like her brother Benedict, left an indelible mark on the Church. Her legacy continues in the many religious communities that trace their lineage to the

Benedictine Rule, reminding us of the power of prayer and the sanctity of dedicated spiritual communion.

PART III

MIRACULA

Amen, amen, I say to you, whoever believes in me will do the works that I do...

Jesus, John 14:12

12

RESURRECTION OF A MONK

Saint Benedict's spiritual gifts extended beyond his teachings and the rule he created for his monks, encompassing a wide range of prophetic, visionary, and miraculous phenomena.

These miracles added to Benedict's reputation for sanctity during his life, contributed to his veneration as a saint after his death, and continue to reinforce the faith of believers in the power of God's intervention in human lives.

Throughout his life, Benedict was said to have performed numerous miracles, as recounted by St. Gregory the Great in his "Dialogues."

The Resurrection of a Young Monk is a particularly amazing story surrounding Benedict's miraculous power. Having been passed down through centuries, this tale was first recorded by Pope St. Gregory the Great in his Dialogues, a series of writings on the lives of early saints.

One day, a monk who was assigned to garden duties accidentally sliced off his own foot with a hoe while working. Hearing the cries of the monk, others quickly came to his aid, bringing the severed foot to Benedict.

Benedict took the severed foot and the suffering monk into the oratory. He ordered the others to leave them, and he shut the door. With the injured man and the detached foot lying before him, Benedict began to pray. He prayed fervently, calling upon the healing power of Christ.

As Benedict prayed, the miraculous happened: the foot was reattached, and there was no trace of the severe injury. The monk was astounded and overwhelmed with joy. He got up, put on his sandals, and returned to his gardening work, perfectly healed.

This miraculous story of Benedict resurrecting the severed foot of the young monk not only testifies to the extraordinary divine powers he was granted but also stands as a testament to his deep faith, prayerful intercession, and compassionate love for his spiritual children. The story underlines the fact that nothing is impossible for God, and that faith and prayer can lead to extraordinary miracles.

13

THE BROKEN SIEVE

The Miracle of the Broken Sieve is one of the earliest tales of Benedict's life, as recounted by St. Gregory the Great in his Dialogues. This event occurred during Benedict's youth while he was still in the village of Enfide (Effide), near Subiaco, before he embarked on his monastic journey.

The story goes that, one day, a servant borrowed a sieve – a utensil used for sifting grain – from a neighboring house. In the course of his duties, the servant accidentally dropped the sieve, causing it to shatter into pieces. Fearful of the repercussions, the servant was overcome with distress.

Seeing the servant's despair, young Benedict, who was not yet fully aware of the divine grace he had been granted, was moved by compassion. He took the broken pieces of the sieve, went to a private place, and began to pray fervently. As he prayed, the sieve miraculously mended itself, with the pieces joining together, leaving no trace of the previous damage.

Benedict returned the perfectly restored sieve to the

stunned servant, thereby relieving him of his distress. The miraculous event, however, began to draw attention and aroused talk among the local villagers. Fearful of the growing attention and seeking to avoid pride, Benedict soon left Enfide, retreating to the solitude of a cave in Subiaco. There, he would grow into the holy man known to us as Benedict, the founder of Western monasticism.

The sieve is said to have been kept at the monastery of Subiaco as a relic, a testimony to this early miracle in the life of Benedict. Through this story, we are reminded of Benedict's compassion, humility, and the divine grace that worked through him, even before his formal commitment to religious life.

14

THE LOAF AND THE GLASS

The Miracle of the Loaf and the Glass is another noteworthy incident in the life of Benedict that displays his divine foresight and miraculous capabilities. As with other episodes from his life, it is captured eloquently in St. Gregory the Great's Dialogues.

The story goes that a certain man sent his servant to Benedict with a flask of wine and a loaf of bread as an offering. Receiving the gifts, Benedict perceived through divine insight that the glass contained not only wine but also a significant danger.

Benedict turned to the servant and said, *"Take care how thou carriest this flask, and see thou dash it not against anything, for it is not whole but cracked, and therefore will not hold the wine."*

The servant, amazed at these words, carefully wrapped the flask in his mantle and started his journey home.

On his way, he stumbled and fell, and the flask struck against a stone, shattering it completely and spilling all the wine. The servant was shocked, recalling Benedict's words, and he marveled at the saint's spiritual insight and prophetic capabilities. He collected the fragments of the flask, returned to his master, and recounted what had transpired.

Meanwhile, the loaf of bread that had also been given as an offering was placed by the brethren in a cupboard, but it mysteriously disappeared. When the matter was brought to Benedict, he simply said, *"The servant who brought it, carried it away again."* And indeed, when they inquired of the servant, they found that this was the truth.

These events further testified to the divine gifts of prophecy and discernment possessed by Benedict, who could perceive hidden realities beyond ordinary human understanding. The tale of the Loaf and the Glass reminds us of Benedict's spiritual insight, his foresight into potential dangers, and his ability to discern truth, even when concealed or far removed from him.

15

THE HEALING OF SERVANDUS

The healing of the Roman patrician Servandus is one of the many miracles associated with Saint St. Benedict of Nursia.

Ranked just below the emperor and his relatives, the patrician families dominated Rome and its empire. As recorded in Pope Gregory the Great's Dialogues, Servandus was suffering from a serious illness which the medical treatments of the time could not cure. In desperation, Servandus sent messengers to Saint Benedict, requesting his prayers.

In response, Benedict sent the patrician a small piece of bread which he had blessed. Upon receiving the bread, Servandus, with faith in the saint's intercession, ate it. Miraculously, his ailment was healed immediately.

Word of this incredible event spread throughout the region, leading many more to seek the prayers and assistance of Saint Benedict, enhancing his reputation as a healer. This episode underscores the profound faith that people had in Saint Benedict and his intercessory power.

The miracle not only enhanced the saint's reputation as

a spiritual figure but also reinforced the belief in divine intervention through the prayers of holy individuals. More importantly, it stands as a testimony to the compassionate nature of Saint Benedict, whose care for the suffering extended beyond the walls of his monastery, reaching out to all those in need, regardless of their status in society.

16

MAURUS AND PLACIDUS

Benedict was known to experience several visions throughout his life, according to St. Gregory the Great's "Dialogues."

One of the most notable visions involved two of his earliest followers, Maurus and Placidus. Both are among the earliest disciples of Benedict and are venerated as saints.

Among the many who were touched by the life and teachings of Saint Benedict, Saint Maurus holds a unique place. Maurus, known for his obedience and devotion, was a close disciple of Saint Benedict and is considered the first and one of the most significant followers of the Benedictine tradition. His life and work reflect the richness of the Benedictine spiritual legacy and exemplify the transformative power of a life devoted to God's service.

Saint Maurus was born in the early 6th century into a noble Roman family. His father, Eutychius, was a senator, and his mother was said to be a virtuous woman of faith. At a young age, Maurus was entrusted to Benedict at Subiaco to be raised in the monastic life, a practice not uncommon among noble families of the time.

St. Maurus became a devoted follower of Benedict, embracing the Rule of St. Benedict in its fullness. Maurus is often depicted in iconography saving Placidus from drowning, a miraculous event described below.

Saint Placidus, like Maurus, holds a unique and cherished place in the annals of Benedictine tradition. A devoted disciple of Saint Benedict, his life is emblematic of the transformative potential of obedience and trust in God.

Placidus was born into a noble Roman family in the early 6th century. His father, the patrician Tertullus, was a man of considerable influence in Rome. In a tradition common among the nobility of the time, Tertullus entrusted his son to Saint Benedict at Subiaco to be trained in the monastic way of life. Thus, at a very tender age, Placidus entered the monastic community under the guidance of Benedict.

Not long after joining the community, however, Placidus became the central figure in a miracle attributed to the power of Benedict's prayer and Maurus' obedience.

17

MIRACLE IN THE LAKE

The most significant event in Placidus's life occurred while he was just a young boy and still adjusting to his new monastic life under Benedict,

One day, Placidus went to fetch water from a lake. Reaching in, he slipped and fell into the turbulent waters and was swept away by the swift current. At this moment, Saint Benedict was away in prayer. However, in a miraculous vision, he saw the incident and called upon Maurus to save Placidus.

Obediently, Maurus ran to the spot and walked upon the water as if on solid ground, reaching out to the drowning Placidus and pulling him out by the hair. This remarkable event demonstrated not only the power of obedience to the monastic rule but also the protective care of God over those who dedicate their lives to His service.

His miraculous rescue is often depicted in art and serves as a powerful testament to the divine protection and guidance offered to those who commit themselves to the service of God.

Placidus' miraculous rescue, as recounted in the Dialogues of Pope St. Gregory the Great, is one of the most enduring stories connected with the early days of the Benedictine Order.

18

FROM MIRACLE TO MARTYR

F ollowing this miraculous event, Placidus continued
to live under the guidance of Benedict, growing in
virtue and commitment to the monastic life. Eventually, he was sent to Sicily, where he founded a monastery.
However, his life was cut short by an attack from local
pirates in which he and his brother monks were martyred.

Despite his short time on earth, Saint Placidus's influence in the Benedictine tradition is profound. His story
serves as an enduring reminder of the power of faith,
obedience, and trust in God's providence, core elements of
the Rule of Saint Benedict. His life and martyrdom also
underscore the dedication and sacrifices made by those
who have chosen to follow the monastic path, spreading
the Gospel message even in the face of persecution and
death.

Likewise, Maurus lived a life of prayer, manual labor,
and communal living as dictated by the Rule. His strict
adherence to the Rule made him a model of Benedictine
spirituality, illustrating the transformative power of prayer,
obedience, and humility.

One of the most significant aspects of Maurus's life, aside from the miracle involving Placidus and Benedict, was his mission to Gaul (modern-day France). At the request of Bishop St. Irenaeus of Lyons, Benedict sent Maurus to establish a monastery in Gaul. Thus, Maurus and his fellow monks founded the Abbey of Glanfeuil, which became a vibrant center of monastic life. Maurus served as the abbot until his death in 584.

Through his role as the first disciple of Benedict and as the first missionary of the Benedictine tradition, Maurus played a pivotal role in establishing the principles of Benedictine monasticism that would eventually spread throughout Europe and the world. His life story underscores the foundational principles of Benedictine spirituality—obedience, humility, and a balance of prayer and work.

Though they lived over a millennium ago, the intertwined stories of Maurus and Placidus continue to inspire and guide those who follow in the footsteps of Saint Benedict.

19

A FLAMING LIGHT

The Vision of a Flaming Light is one of the most profound spiritual experiences in the life of Benedict, illustrating his deep connection to God and his mystical insights into the spiritual realm. This vision, as documented by Pope St. Gregory the Great in his "Dialogues," is an illuminating testament to Benedict's sanctity and spiritual discernment.

As St. Gregory tells it, one night, Benedict was alone in prayer when suddenly, he experienced a divine illumination. It was as if the darkness of the night had been driven away, replaced by a flood of brilliant light. In this overwhelming radiance, he had a mystical vision where he seemed to be transported outside of himself.

In this vision, the entire world was laid before him, gathered together, as he described it, "in a single ray of light." This wasn't merely a geographical understanding but a deeply spiritual one - seeing the world bound together in the unity of God's creation, interconnected through the divine light of God's presence.

Simultaneously, he beheld the soul of Germanus, the

bishop of Capua, being carried to heaven by angels. He immediately sent word to the monastic brethren of the bishop's passing, which was confirmed a few days later when messengers from Capua arrived to report the news.

This mystical experience of the Flaming Light not only further confirmed Benedict's sanctity but also provided a beautiful imagery of the divine omniscience and omnipresence. It showed that in God, all of creation is intimately connected, and that in His light, there is the illumination of spiritual understanding beyond the boundaries of physical distance and earthly life.

20

THE PATH TO GOD

B enedict's vision of the path to God, recounted in St. Gregory the Great's "Dialogues", is one of the saint's most profound mystical experiences, revealing the connection between earthly life and heavenly destiny.

While in prayer one night in his monastery at Monte Cassino, Benedict was granted a divine vision. Suddenly, his inner sight was illumined, and he saw a single radiant path stretching up towards the heavens. This pathway, glowing like a ray of light, cut through the opaque darkness of the night, presenting a clear path from earth to heaven.

In his vision, he saw that this path was not empty. Ascending the path were the souls of monks, their bodies not restricted by earthly gravity, climbing toward their heavenly home. This was a visual representation of the spiritual journey, the progress of souls toward their ulti-mate end in God.

However, the ascent was not the same for every soul. Some seemed to climb the radiant path with ease, their progress swift and assured. These represented those who, in life, had committed themselves fully to the commands of God and the teachings of the Church. Their dedication to prayer, penance, and charity had prepared them well for their heavenly ascent.

Others on the path struggled. Their progress was slow, their climb laborious. This showed that their journey to God in life had been marked by struggle, by sin and repentance, by a battle against their earthly desires. Yet, they too were making their way up the path, demonstrating the power of God's mercy and the possibility of redemption and spiritual growth even amidst struggles.

At the top of the radiant path stood Christ Himself, bathed in glorious light. He stood not as a distant judge, but as a welcoming savior, His arms open wide in a gesture of eternal acceptance. His presence was a reassurance of the promise of eternal life, a beacon guiding those on their arduous spiritual journey.

This vision deeply influenced Benedict and affirmed the spiritual direction he provided to his monks. It underlined the importance of monastic discipline and perseverance in the spiritual journey, symbolized by the ascent along the radiant path. The vision also offered a powerful image of hope, emphasizing that Christ is always waiting to welcome souls at the end of their earthly journey. It continues to inspire followers of the Benedictine Rule and the wider Christian community to this day.

Another notable divine experience involved the death of his twin sister, St. Scholastica, and a vision which confirmed her sanctity and union with God in the afterlife.

These visions bear testimony to the deep spiritual insights of Benedict and his close communion with the divine. They guided him throughout his life, and they continue to inspire and teach those who follow his Rule today.

21

THE MONASTERY PROPHECY

Benedict is known to have been given the gift of prophecy. According to the accounts of his life recorded by St. Gregory the Great in his *Dialogues*, Benedict could read the hearts of people, predict future events, and experienced visions of things happening far away.

For example, Benedict prophesied that his disciples, at the Monastery of Monte Cassino, would live according to his Rule until the end of the world, and that his monastery would suffer severe tribulation. Indeed, the Monastery of Monte Cassino has experienced destruction and persecution multiple times, but each time it has been rebuilt and the Benedictine Order continues to thrive today.

The prophecy regarding the future of his monastery is a testament to Benedict's gift of foresight and his profound understanding of the spiritual and worldly challenges his community would face. This story is primarily sourced from the Dialogues of St. Gregory the Great.

It is said that one day, Benedict was in deep contemplation when he was granted a divine vision. In it, he foresaw the future destruction of his monastery at Monte Cassino. He saw that the monks would be dispersed, the buildings leveled, and all the hard work of the community undone. This devastation would be wrought by the hands of wicked men.

Despite the sorrow this vision must have caused him, Benedict did not hide this prophecy from his community. He shared it with the monks so they would be spiritually prepared for the trials to come. In this, we see Benedict's belief in the importance of resilience and faith in the face of adversity.

True to the saint's prophecy, the monastery of Monte Cassino was destroyed multiple times over the centuries. It was first sacked by the Lombards around 581 AD, nearly a century after Benedict's death, then by the Saracens in 884 AD, and finally, the monastery was bombed during World War II in February 1944.

Each time, just as Benedict had foreseen, the monks were scattered, the buildings were ruined, but they always returned. They rebuilt the monastery and continued their work, carrying on the spiritual legacy of their founder. Today, Monte Cassino stands rebuilt and active, an enduring symbol of the Benedictine motto: "Succisa Virescit" – "When cut down, it grows back stronger." This was exactly as Benedict had prophesied – a testament to his foresight and the enduring spirit of the Benedictine community.

22

EXCOMMUNICATED MONKS

When Benedict excommunicated a few monks for disobedience, he prophesied that they would die outside the monastery. This came to pass as the disobedient monks died in an accident outside the monastery.

The story of Benedict's prophecy regarding the death of excommunicated monks showcases his spiritual insight and a symbol of the negative effects of disobedience to God. This tale is sourced from the Dialogues of St. Gregory the Great.

In his community at Monte Cassino, there were a few monks who continuously disregarded Benedict's Rule, sowing discord and refusing to amend their ways despite repeated admonitions. For the sake of maintaining the harmony and spiritual focus of the community, Benedict eventually found it necessary to excommunicate these monks.

However, instead of being chastened by this serious action, these monks departed and continued to lead lives of disobedience and irreverence. It was then that Benedict

had a prophetic vision. He saw the souls of these excommunicated monks being carried away in a fiery chariot, a
symbol of their impending death and damnation.

A few days later, the prophecy came true. Word reached
the monastery that the excommunicated monks had
perished. It was a sobering moment for the entire community, serving as a stark reminder of the consequences of
persisting in disobedience and not seeking reconciliation
with the church and God.

Through this tragic event, Benedict's prophecy underlined the importance of maintaining discipline within the
community and seeking a path of repentance and reconciliation when one strays from it. The tale illustrates his
commitment to guiding his monks towards a righteous
path and his profound sorrow when any of them were lost
to sin.

23

THE WAYWARD MONK

The account of Benedict's prophecy about The Wayward Monk underscores his deep spiritual insight and his understanding of the challenges inherent in the spiritual life. This account is derived from St. Gregory the Great's Dialogues.

One day, a monk from another monastery came to visit Benedict. The monk, desiring to lead a hermit's life, sought advice from the wise Benedict. Benedict, discerning the spiritual dangers the monk would face, warned him against such a venture. He prophetically told the monk that he would be severely tempted by the devil, to the point of being drawn away from his hermitage and back to his old monastic community.

The monk, believing in his own spiritual strength, ignored Benedict's counsel and withdrew into the wilderness. There, he lived a solitary life of prayer and fasting, believing he could resist any temptation that might come his way.

However, Benedict's prophecy came to pass. After a short time in the wilderness, the monk was assailed by severe temptations. In his solitude, the devil tempted him with a severe longing for his old monastic life. Unable to bear the spiritual struggle, the monk eventually left the wilderness and returned to his old monastery, confirming the truth of Benedict's prophetic warning.

This story exemplifies Benedict's profound spiritual discernment and his understanding of the subtleties of the spiritual journey. It serves as a cautionary tale about the seriousness of ascetic endeavors and the necessity of heeding wise spiritual counsel.

These instances, among others, portray Benedict as being deeply in tune with the divine, and his prophetic insights further solidified the deep respect and veneration that his disciples and followers had for him. After many years of hard work, major accomplishments, and plenty of trials and tribulations, Benedict made one final prophecy, this one concerning himself.

24

INSIGHT INTO SIN

Benedict was often granted the spiritual gift of discernment, which allowed him to perceive the sins of others, even those hidden or committed in secret. This was not a vision of divine presence but rather a divine gift that allowed him to guide and admonish his monks effectively.

One such instance is found in St. Gregory the Great's *Dialogues*, which details a striking occurrence demonstrating Benedict's ability to perceive hidden sin.

In one chapter, Gregory describes a monastery governed by an abbot named Isaac. The brothers living there were falling into grave sins of the flesh, but Isaac was unable to perceive or correct these misdeeds. Desperate for guidance, Isaac sought the counsel of Benedict.

Upon his arrival at Benedict's monastery, the holy man immediately addressed Isaac's concerns without having been verbally briefed on the situation. Benedict said to Isaac, *"The faults of thy monks are not hidden from thee, but thou dost connive at them; and what is more serious, thou dost, as it were, by thy silence, strengthen them in their evil deeds."*

Shocked by this revelation, Isaac vehemently denied having been lax in his duties, saying he was completely ignorant of any wrongdoing. Yet Benedict, firm in his spiritual insight, not only insisted on the presence of sin but even indicated that it was occurring during the night hours.

Guided by Benedict's revelation, Isaac returned to his monastery and kept a vigilant watch over his monks. Just as Benedict had foretold, he discovered the sinful conduct of some of his monks, which had been hidden from him but not from the divine perception of Benedict.

This is one of many instances where Benedict was able to discern sin in others, even from afar. His gift of insight was a critical tool in his mission to guide and correct those under his care, always leading them toward holiness and away from the snares of sin.

Through his God-given spiritual discernment, he was able to address not only overt sins but also those sins which were hidden and unconfessed, contributing to the spiritual health and growth of his monastic communities.

25

THE IDLE BOY

A nother impressive demonstration of Benedict's gift of Insight into Sin is the story of a young boy entrusted to the care of the monks at Subiaco.

In the Dialogues of St. Gregory the Great, it is written that a certain man from the city decided to offer his son to God and placed him under the care of Benedict at the monastery. The boy lived obediently for a while, but with time, he began to loathe the discipline and hard work, longing for a more carefree life.

One day, the boy secretly left the monastery, going down to the village to enjoy himself in idleness. When Benedict realized the boy had fled, he called for Maurus, his trusted disciple. He told him, *"Brother Maurus, run quickly, for the boy who has gone away from here has descended to the plain below, and at this very moment, he is sitting and eating in a house with other idlers. Go, I say, lest while he is eating, he may lose his soul."*

Maurus, startled by this revelation, ran as swiftly as he could to the village. Indeed, he found the boy sitting at a table just as Benedict had described, ready to partake in a meal.

Maurus, reprimanding him for his disobedience, brought him back to the monastery. The boy was filled with remorse for his actions, and from then on, he was obedient, disciplined, and committed to his monastic duties.

This event speaks to Benedict's profound spiritual discernment, his Insight into Sin. He was not only able to perceive the boy's physical location but also his spiritual endangerment. This gift of discernment aided him in the governance of his monastery and the spiritual guidance of the monks under his care, leading them back to the path of righteousness whenever they strayed.

26

BENEDICT'S HOLY DEATH

B enedict passed away around 547 AD. His death is
shrouded in a sacred aura, depicted in the second
book of the "Dialogues" by Pope St. Gregory the
Great, the primary source for information about the life of
Benedict.

According to St. Gregory, Benedict foresaw his own
death. He informed his disciples of his impending departure six days in advance and asked them to dig a grave.
During those days, he gave his final instructions and
farewells.

In the last moments of his life, Benedict asked to be
brought to the chapel. Supported by his monks, he received
the Body and Blood of Christ in the Eucharist and then
raised his hands in prayer while standing. As he uttered his
last prayer, he died, standing in the chapel, supported in
the arms of his disciples. This occurred on March 21, 547
AD, and he was buried next to his sister, St. Scholastica, at
the Abbey of Monte Cassino.

The manner of Benedict's death - in prayer, after
receiving the Eucharist - reflects his life's work of seeking

God through monasticism. His final act was a testament to the monastic ideals he promoted: prayer, work, and community life.

Benedict's death is remembered in the Benedictine world with solemnity and reverence, acknowledging the significant impact of his monastic Rule, which continues to guide monastic life even today.

PART IV

DIABOLUS

Begone Satan! Never tempt me with your vanities! What you offer me is evil. Drink the poison yourself!

St. Benedict Medal inscription

27

PATRON OF EXORCISTS

B enedict is perhaps best known as the founder of Western Monasticism and the author of the Rule that bears his name. However, the power and reach of Benedict extend far beyond his work with monastic communities.

His life, as recorded in Pope Gregory the Great's Dialogues, paints a compelling portrait of Benedict as a stalwart soldier in spiritual warfare, an exorcist who continually battled demonic forces, casting out evil spirits and providing succor to the afflicted.

The first such account comes from within his own monastic community. A monk, who could not keep still during communal prayer, seemed constantly disturbed by an invisible presence. He would often leave the oratory and go outside to wander amongst the bushes, looking up at the sky and allowing his mind to drift.

Benedict observed this monk's habitual distraction and warned him about his behavior, urging him to remain with the others during prayer. Despite the warning, the monk was unable to change his ways.

Finally, Benedict decided to personally observe the monk during prayer. He saw a small, dark figure pulling the monk away from prayer and leading him outside. Recognizing this figure as a demon, and seeing the distress it was causing, Benedict followed the monk outside. With a prayer and a sign of the cross, he commanded the demon to depart.

The monk was immediately freed of his restlessness, a clear instance of Benedict's power to exorcise evil spirits tormenting the faithful. Afterward, the monk was no longer troubled by this urge to leave during prayer, and he was able to remain in the oratory with his brothers.

The story is a testament to Benedict's discernment. His ability to see the invisible influence of evil and his readiness to intervene for the spiritual good of his brothers epitomizes his deep spiritual insight.

A more pronounced exorcism is recounted where a desperate father sought out Benedict, his son writhing in the grips of demonic possession. Benedict prayed fervently over the young boy and, with the sign of the cross, expelled the tormenting demon. This singular act of exorcism, a clear assertion of spiritual authority over the diabolical, provided immediate relief and restored the boy's health.

Benedict's power of exorcism was not confined to individuals. Upon his arrival at Monte Cassino, he was faced with a temple believed to be inhabited by a demon. Undeterred, Benedict entered this pagan place of worship and prayed fervently, his sacred power overwhelming the dark inhabitant of the temple. The demon was cast out, and the once pagan temple was transformed into a Christian chapel.

However, the spiritual battles of Benedict were not limited to exorcism alone. He continually contended with forces of evil in a variety of contexts. His triumphs over the attempts to poison him, for example—once by a jealous cleric, Florentius, and another time by a group of rebellious monks—turned into testaments of his spiritual strength.

Benedict's battles against evil forces solidify his position as a spiritual warrior and an exorcist, reinforcing his deep devotion to God and his unwavering stand against the forces of evil. As we don his medal and invoke his intercession today, we recall Benedict, not only as the Patron of Europe or the founder of Western monasticism but also as the holy exorcist, a valiant soldier in the spiritual battlefield, ever ready to intercede on our behalf in our own battles against evil.

28

TRIAL IN THE WILDERNESS

Benedict's encounters with evil, as recorded by St. Gregory the Great in his "Dialogues", show the saint's spiritual strength and his capacity to confront and resist demonic powers. These experiences are key in understanding why Benedict is often invoked in the Church's spiritual warfare and exorcism prayers.

The story of Benedict's Temptation in the Wilderness serves as a powerful testament to the struggles he underwent in his pursuit of holiness, reminiscent of Christ's own temptations in the desert. This narrative is sourced from the Dialogues of St. Gregory the Great, a rich depository of early Benedictine tradition.

As the story goes, while living in solitude in a cave at Subiaco, young Benedict was subject to an intense onslaught of temptation. Having cut himself off from the world to focus on prayer and contemplation, he was not insulated from the machinations of the devil. One day, he was overcome by the memory of a woman he had once known in Rome. The vivid recollection stirred up such strong passions in him that he was on the brink of abandoning his hermitage.

In the heat of this battle, inspired by divine guidance, Benedict acted decisively. He stripped off his clothing and threw himself into a patch of thorny brambles and nettles. His body lacerated by the thorns, the physical pain served to quell the surge of lustful thoughts. It was a symbolic act, with the thorns piercing his flesh representing the painful but necessary mortification required to overcome the lures of the flesh.

From that day forward, it is said, he was never again troubled by such temptation. He had won a decisive victory over his own passions and demonstrated an extreme commitment to the monastic vows of chastity and purity. This experience profoundly shaped Benedict and his spiritual teaching, instilling in him a keen understanding of the internal struggles that come with a commitment to a holy life.

The narrative of Benedict's Temptation in the Wilderness remains a powerful reminder of the spiritual warfare that individuals committed to a life of piety and virtue often face, and the lengths to which one may have to go to guard against the snares of the devil.

29

BLACKBIRD OF TEMPTATION

The story of Benedict and the Blackbird of Temptation is a fascinating tale of spiritual warfare and divine grace. It is found in the Dialogues of St. Gregory the Great, a significant source of information about the life and miracles of Benedict.

According to St. Gregory, there came a time during Benedict's solitary existence in the cave at Subiaco when he was assaulted by a violent temptation of the flesh. The enemy of human nature, the devil, sought to disturb his devoted heart with the memory of a woman he had seen in the past, causing a fierce arousal within him.

Just when the temptation seemed overwhelming, a blackbird appeared before him. Benedict watched the bird closely as it flew in circles around him and then quickly away. The sudden and close presence of the bird served as a wake-up call, breaking the spell of temptation that had gripped him.

Seeing this as a sign from God, Benedict instantly regained his spiritual alertness and began to pray fervently. His prayer was so intense that he felt as if a fire was raging within him, a divine heat that scorched and eradicated the illicit desires instigated by the devil.

Having prayed, Benedict found himself freed from the fiery darts of temptation. The small blackbird, thus, came to symbolize the temptations that can circle and strike without warning. But more importantly, it also signified the grace of God that can suddenly intervene, giving the strength to resist and overcome.

This story remains a profound allegory in Christian spirituality, reminding believers of the relentless spiritual struggles they may face, but more importantly, of the transforming power of prayer and God's ever-present help in times of temptation.

30

THE ROLLING STONE

The story of Benedict and The Rolling Stone is another fascinating tale from the Dialogues of St. Gregory the Great, highlighting the saint's gift of miraculous intercession and the power of faith.

As the narrative goes, during the construction of the monastery at Monte Cassino, the monks were attempting to move a large stone for the building work. Despite their collective efforts, the stone remained immovable. It was as if some unseen force held the boulder in place.

Perplexed and discouraged, the monks turned to Benedict for guidance, explaining the unusual nature of their predicament. Responding to their distress, Benedict approached the obstinate rock and offered a prayer.

Having finished his prayer, he ordered the monks to try moving the stone again. To their amazement, what was previously an impossible task became incredibly easy. The stone, which had refused to budge, now moved as if it was weightless. The monks, filled with awe, praised the glory of God and the holiness of Benedict.

This miracle, as recounted by St. Gregory, is an

enduring testament to the power of prayer and faith, and the divine intervention that can remove even the most formidable obstacles in our lives. It is a story that continues to inspire the Benedictine community and believers worldwide, reminding them of the promise found in the Gospel, *"If you have faith as small as a mustard seed, you can say to this mountain, 'Move from here to there,' and it will move" (Matthew 17:20).*

31

DEVIL IN DISGUISE

High upon a windswept hill stood the monastery, its stone walls echoing with chants and prayers. Yet, within its hallowed walls, a sinister shadow had begun to loom.

One day, as the aging St. Benedict journeyed along the rugged path away from the monastery, the devil hatched his insidious plan. He transformed into an elderly monk, his visage a cunning mask of benevolence, his eyes flickering with an eerie light.

Simultaneously, a physician had been summoned to the monastery, bearing in his satchel remedies for the ailing monks. As the doctor approached, the cloaked figure of the devil intercepted him on the monastery's outer fringes.

With a voice as smooth as polished stone, he identified himself as one of the monks, requesting the medicine to bring to his ailing brothers. The physician, seeing nothing amiss in the gentle demeanor of the elderly monk, complied and handed over the healing elixirs.

All the while, Benedict, guided by divine insight, was engaged in fervent prayer. His spirit, ever attuned to the spectral undercurrents, detected the devil's deceit. A rush of adrenaline coursed through him, his heart pounded in his chest like a war drum, and he knew he must act swiftly to avert impending disaster.

Charging back to the monastery, his robe billowing in the wind, Benedict crossed paths with the devil in disguise. The devil, appearing as the elderly monk, was poised to distribute the tainted medicine, his eyes gleaming with wicked anticipation. But Benedict, empowered by divine force, recognized the malevolent spirit beneath the guise.

With a firm hand, he shoved the disguised devil, his voice echoing through the hallowed halls, "Be gone, deceiver!" The elderly monk's form crumpled, and with a final shudder, the devil was expelled, leaving behind an astounded monk, freed from the grasp of evil.

From that day forward, the tale of St. Benedict's confrontation with the devil was recounted in hushed whispers, further reinforcing his title as the Patron Saint of Exorcists.

32

VISION OF EVIL

St. Gregory the Great recounts a striking vision experienced by Benedict in his "Dialogues", which vividly illustrates the spiritual warfare faced by souls on their path to heaven. This vision is known as the Vision of Evil Spirits.

One night, while at prayer, Benedict received a profound spiritual insight. His interior sight, or the eyes of his soul, were opened, and he was granted a vision that encompassed the entire world as if under a single ray of sunlight. This global illumination represented the enlightenment of divine knowledge, where the mysteries of the universe were suddenly made clear to him.

In this divinely illuminated sight, Benedict saw a great and diverse multitude ascending toward heaven. These represented the souls of monks, striving toward union with God. They were climbing a ladder, an echo of Jacob's ladder from the Old Testament, where Jacob saw angels ascending and descending between heaven and earth. Here, the monks were the ones ascending, working their way upward toward heavenly glory.

However, the vision was not just of peaceful ascension. As the monks climbed, Benedict saw that they were not alone. Evil spirits, symbolizing demonic powers, were also present. These malicious entities were trying to drag the monks down, pulling at them in an attempt to hinder their ascent.

Some monks seemed to shrug off these attacks with ease, their firm resolve and deep faith keeping them from being drawn away. Others struggled, torn between their heavenly calling and the earthly temptations represented by the demonic figures. Despite the spiritual warfare unfolding, the vision was not one of despair, for Benedict also saw that the monks were not without aid.

The figure of Christ stood at the top of the ladder, watching over the monks as they made their perilous ascent. With His presence, He offered a beacon of hope, guidance, and the promise of ultimate victory for those who persevere.

This vision gave Benedict profound insight into the spiritual struggles his monks, and indeed all Christians, face in their journey towards holiness. It reinforced his commitment to guiding them through their battles with temptation and solidified the spiritual warfare aspects of his Rule, which to this day serves as a roadmap for individuals striving for sanctity.

These experiences depict Benedict as a spiritual warrior who faced evil powers and emerged victorious. As such, he is often invoked for protection against evil and is held up as a model of spiritual resilience. The St. Benedict Medal carries inscriptions that refer to these struggles, and it is often used as a tangible means of seeking his powerful intercession for protection against evil.

33

SPIRITUAL WARFARE

Benedict has long been invoked in the Church in the context of spiritual warfare and exorcism, a practice that likely stems from accounts of his own confrontations with evil forces during his lifetime. The power of Benedict against evil is symbolically expressed in the St. Benedict Medal, which contains inscriptions for protection and the casting out of evil.

It's important to note that exorcisms are private, confidential rituals in the Catholic Church, often treated with the utmost discretion and respect for the privacy of the individuals involved. Specifics of such rites, including any eyewitness accounts, are not usually disclosed publicly.

However, it's widely known that Benedict is a commonly invoked saint in rites of exorcism, and the St. Benedict Medal is considered to have protective properties against evil. According to numerous public, general testimonies and writings, Benedict and his medal have been integral in the Church's fight against evil, and many exorcists continue to utilize them in their spiritual warfare.

The Church's exorcists, in their mission to liberate the

possessed from the influence of evil spirits, are known to call upon the intercession of Benedict, recognizing his particular authority in the face of demonic forces. They utilize prayers associated with Benedict, most notably the Exorcism Prayer on the Medal of Benedict:

"Vade retro Satana! Nunquam suade mihi vana! Sunt mala quae libas. Ipse venena bibas!"

In English, this translates to *"Begone Satan! Never tempt me with your vanities! What you offer me is evil. Drink the poison yourself!"*

While the Medal of Benedict is not an amulet or a magical charm but a symbol of faith, exorcists and the faithful alike often use it as a physical point of focus for invoking Benedict's protection and intercession.

In addition to the medal, the prayer of Benedict is also utilized in exorcism practices. This prayer is a powerful invocation asking for the saint's intercession in the battle against evil forces. An example of a prayer that might be used by an exorcist is as follows:

"Benedict, you were a man of peace in the midst of a world of war and a man of hope in a world of despair. You resisted the temptations of the devil and gained strength from the Bread of Life. Help us to resist the snares of the devil and his minions in every form of evil which presents itself to us. Strengthen us in our weakness and guide us in our efforts to follow Jesus Christ and to share in His eternal glory. Amen."

Exorcists may also use other prayers that call upon Benedict, such as the following:

"O Glorious Benedict, sublime model of all virtues, pure vessel of God's grace! Behold me, humbly kneeling at your feet. I implore your loving heart to pray for me before the throne of God. To you, I have recourse in all the dangers which daily surround me. Shield me against my enemies, inspire me to imitate you in all things. May your blessing be with me

always, so that I may shun whatever God forbids and avoid the occasions of sin."

The following prayer, part of the Rite of Exorcism, does not specifically mention Benedict, but it represents the kind of invocative prayers that exorcists might employ during an exorcism:

"In the Name of Jesus Christ, our God and Lord, strengthened by the intercession of the Immaculate Virgin Mary, Mother of God, of Blessed Michael the Archangel, of the Blessed Apostles Peter and Paul and all the Saints, [and powerful in the holy authority of our ministry], we confidently undertake to repulse the attacks and deceits of the devil."

While Benedict is not named specifically in this prayer, his intercession can be invoked during the *"[and powerful in the holy authority of our ministry]"* part of the prayer, given his well-known reputation for combating evil and his role as a protector against demonic influence.

While exorcists often invoke the intercession of Benedict, it's important to note that the Church teaches that all authority over demons ultimately comes from Christ. The prayers, sacraments, and sacramentals of the Church, including those associated with Benedict, are aids that work within the framework of a life oriented towards Christ and are not substitutes for a deep, personal relationship with Him.

34

THE BENEDICTINE REBUKE

"*Vade retro satana,*" a Latin phrase translated to English as *"Get behind me, Satan,"* is known to Catholics worldwide as a powerful rebuke to the devil. It first gained formal recognition as an exorcism formula in the Middle Ages, and a key source for its early usage comes from a 1415 manuscript found in Metten Abbey, a Benedictine monastery in Bavaria, Germany.

Metten Abbey, founded in 766 AD, has a rich Benedictine heritage and has survived through the centuries as a place of prayer, work, and study, true to the Benedictine motto *"ora et labora" (pray and work).* The discovery of this manuscript in Metten Abbey reveals a significant chapter in the history of Catholic exorcisms and the role of the Benedictines in preserving and propagating spiritual tools against evil.

The 1415 manuscript describes an early form of the St. Benedict Medal, which was then simply a cross with the initials of certain words inscribed. According to the manuscript, the cross was inscribed with the Latin exorcism formula *"Crux sacra sit mihi lux! Nunquam draco sit mihi dux"* ("May the holy cross be my light! May the dragon never be my guide!").

The phrase *"Vade retro satana"* is part of the larger inscriptive formula, which also includes the abbreviated invocation *"V.R.S.N.S.M.V - S.M.Q.L.I.V.B."*, standing for *"Vade retro satana, nunquam suade mihi vana — sunt mala quae libas, ipse venena bibas"* ("Get behind me Satan, never suggest vain thoughts to me — the cup you offer is evil, drink your own poison").

In the context of medieval exorcism, these formulas were not simply words but weapons in the spiritual battle against demonic forces. Such invocations offered a way for the faithful to assert their belief in God's power over evil. The connection of *"Vade retro satana"* to Benedict, and its presence in a manuscript housed in a Benedictine monastery, underscores Benedict's enduring legacy in the Church's spiritual warfare.

These exorcism formulas have become intrinsically linked to Benedict's legacy and are a testament to his life-long struggle against evil. The discovery of the Metten manuscript allowed for the wider recognition of the St. Benedict Medal and its inscriptions, establishing its reputation as a potent sacramental against demonic influence.

The Benedict that most people know today, however, features even more powerful imagery and symbolism.

ST. BENEDICT MEDAL

35

THE ST. BENEDICT MEDAL

From biblical underpinnings to a tangible sacramental, the St. Benedict Medal evolved over the centuries to become one of the oldest and most respected sacramentals of the Catholic Church.

The medal's form and usage have gone through slight changes, but its core purpose has remained the same: a physical reminder of the Christian's spiritual combat against evil, a token of devotion to Benedict, and, according to many of the Church's exorcists, a powerful form of divine protection.

While the St. Benedict Medal itself did not exist in biblical times, its roots are deeply biblical. Its front bears the image of Benedict holding a cross, symbolizing the power of Christ's sacrifice and the faith in His triumph over evil—themes fundamental to Christianity from its inception.

The reverse side carries significant inscriptions, including *"Vade retro satana"* (*"Get behind me, Satan"*), echoing Christ's rebuke of Peter in the Gospel of Mark (8:33):

At this he turned around and, looking at his disciples, rebuked Peter and said, "Get behind me, Satan. You are thinking not as God does, but as human beings do."

The evolution into the form that we recognize today started in the Middle Ages. An early precursor to the medal was a cross, believed to have been owned by Benedict. The exact form and inscriptions varied, but the cross often bore the initials of certain Latin prayers, serving as a reminder of the Christian's continual struggle against evil and the call to live according to Christ's teachings.

The next major milestone in the evolution of the St. Benedict Medal took place in the early 17th century. A manuscript dating back to 1415 was discovered in Metten Abbey, a Benedictine monastery in Bavaria, Germany.

This manuscript provided a detailed explanation of the inscriptions on the Benedict cross, most notably the abbreviation: *"V.R.S.N.S.M.V. - S.M.Q.L.I.V.B."*

This stands for *"Vade retro satana, nunquam suade mihi vana — sunt mala quae libas, ipse venena bibas"* ("Get behind me Satan, never suggest vain thoughts to me — the cup you offer is evil, drink your own poison").

Following the discovery at Metten Abbey, the use of the medal spread, and the medal took on the form we recognize today. In 1741, Pope Benedict XIV approved the use and inscriptions of the St. Benedict Medal, promoting its pious use throughout the Church.

Today, the St. Benedict Medal is revered as a powerful sacramental, used for invoking spiritual protection and intercession from Benedict. Many Catholics wear the medal or carry it with them, often incorporated into rosaries or other religious items. The medal is also often affixed to the foundations of buildings or entrances to homes as a spiritual safeguard.

In the face of life's spiritual challenges, the St. Benedict

Medal serves as a silent prayer and testament of faith, embodying the believer's rejection of evil and steadfast commitment to Christ.

ST. BENEDICT MEDAL

36

THE DEVIL'S BRIDGE

The early thirteenth century was an era of whispers and shadowy folklore in the French town of Sens.

One such tale that continued to echo through the narrow, cobbled streets involved an ambitious architect, a contract inked in blood, and an encounter with the Devil himself that forever transformed the landscape of the town.

The architect, whose identity has been washed away by the currents of time, had been commissioned to construct a bridge over the river Yonne. Despite his unquestionable skill, the complexity of the project brought him to his knees, leaving him desperate and vulnerable. In his desperation, he found himself at a dangerous crossroads. A pact with the Devil.

The Devil, always keen on exploiting human weaknesses, agreed to complete the bridge in return for the architect's soul, a timeless currency in such perilous deals. With the completion of the grand bridge, the architect's sense of accomplishment soon turned into a dread-filled realization of the price he was to pay.

In his fear and desperation, the architect sought the counsel of M. le Curé of Sens. A compassionate man, the Curé was renowned for his piety and unwavering faith. Hearing the architect's plea, he agreed to help, vowing to use every weapon in his spiritual arsenal.

Standing on the majestic structure, the Curé called upon the divine power of St. Benedict, reciting the potent exorcism prayer. The air thickened, and a deafening silence descended upon the scene as he intoned, *"Crux sacra sit mihi lux! Nunquam draco sit mihi dux!"* which, in English, translates to *"May the holy cross be my light! May the dragon never be my guide!"*

The bridge quaked beneath their feet, and a deafening roar echoed through the air, a final act of defiance before the Devil's grasp on the architect's soul shattered, banishing him back into the shadowy depths from whence he came. The architect fell to his knees, a free man once again, his soul redeemed by the power of the St. Benedict's prayer and the Curé's unwavering faith.

This encounter etched itself into the annals of Sens as a potent testament to the power of faith and redemption, leaving behind not only a marvel of architecture but also an enduring legend of the battle between good and evil. The architect's bridge, now known as the Devil's Bridge, stands as a stark reminder of the forces that once wrestled upon it, a silent testament to St. Benedict's power over evil.

37

THE TRUE CROSS

The Blessing of St. Maur, a long-standing tradition within the Benedictine Order, holds a special place in the hearts of the faithful.

Originally, the blessing was customarily bestowed upon the sick using a relic of the True Cross, with the sincere hope of assisting in the swift recovery of their health. The True Cross, believed to be remnants of the cross upon which Jesus was crucified, has been venerated as one of the most significant relics in Christianity, and its use in the blessing conferred an extraordinary spiritual significance.

However, as the centuries wore on, it became increasingly challenging to obtain a relic of the True Cross for the purposes of conferring the Blessing of St. Maur. Recognizing the importance of this blessing, the Sacred Congregation of Rites, a body of the Roman Curia that governed Catholic liturgical practices, sought a solution to ensure that this vital ministry could continue unhindered.

In 1959, the Sacred Congregation of Rites issued a decree that would bring a new dimension to the practice. They granted permission for St. Benedict Medals to be used in place of the relic of the True Cross for the Blessing of St. Maur.

The rationale behind this decision was the high regard in which St. Benedict was held, and the medal's widely recognized representation of the saint's intercessory power. This enabled the faithful to continue to confer the blessing despite the scarcity of True Cross relics.

The St. Benedict Medal, imbued with the spirit of St. Benedict's strength, sanctity, and spiritual warfare against evil, thus became a potent symbol in bestowing the Blessing of St. Maur. It served as a tangible reminder of St. Benedict's powerful intercession and the grace conferred by this revered blessing.

This shift not only preserved the tradition of the Blessing of St. Maur but also amplified its connection to St. Benedict, reminding the faithful of his enduring influence and the spiritual potency attributed to his medal.

Today, the Blessing of St. Maur continues to be a cherished practice within the Benedictine Order and among the faithful at large. Its evolution from the use of a relic of the True Cross to the St. Benedict Medal underlines the resilience and adaptability of the Church's traditions in the face of challenges, while also showcasing the remarkable and enduring legacy of St. Benedict.

38

MEDAL OF CONVERSION

P rosper Guéranger, a French Benedictine monk and
liturgist, is best known for his comprehensive work
"The Liturgical Year."

Yet, his lesser-known writings also provide incredible
accounts of religious conversions, many of which he
attributed to the intercession of St. Benedict through the
pious use of the medal.

One such account tells of a staunch atheist scientist,
driven by a desire to disprove the existence of God.
According to Guéranger, the scientist found a St. Benedict
Medal and, though he ridiculed its significance, kept it out
of curiosity. Over time, he found himself inexplicably
drawn to the Church, ultimately leading him to embrace
the Catholic faith.

In a letter cited by Guéranger, the scientist wrote, "In the
reflective silence of my study, I found myself repeatedly gazing
upon that tiny medal... I felt an undeniable stirring, a call to
something beyond the realm of my calculations and
experiments."

Guéranger also recounts the story of a young woman,

trapped in a lifestyle of vice and excess, who received a St. Benedict Medal from a passing stranger. Despite her initial disregard, she eventually found herself moved by an unexplained peace every time she held the medal. As Guéranger quotes her testimony, *"In those moments of quiet with the medal in my hand, I felt seen, not judged but loved, as if gently called back home."*

This transformative experience led her on a path to conversion, recovery, and a newfound dedication to the Church.

In another narrative, Guéranger speaks of a fallen away Catholic who held hostility towards the Church. However, upon the death of a close friend, he received a St. Benedict Medal among the friend's belongings.

Driven by nostalgia and respect for his deceased friend, he kept the medal. Soon after, he experienced a profound spiritual awakening, finding reconciliation with the Church. Guéranger cites his letter stating, *"In the presence of the medal, I felt an irresistible pull towards the faith of my childhood, like a prodigal son yearning for home."*

These anecdotes from Prosper Guéranger serve as profound testimonials to the spiritual transformation attributed to the intercession of St. Benedict through the pious use of his medal.

From staunch atheists to prodigal sons, the veneration of the St. Benedict Medal has been linked with an array of extraordinary conversions, underscoring the enduring power of faith and the miraculous intercession attributed to St. Benedict.

39

DIVINE PROTECTION

The Medal of Benedict is a sacramental medal rich in Christian symbolism and an important component of the saint's enduring legacy. It has been used in the Church for centuries as a means of fostering spiritual devotion and as a protective symbol against evil influences.

Here's a detailed look at the features of the St. Benedict Medal:

The **Front of the Medal:**

- **Image of Benedict:** At the center of the medal is Benedict, holding a cross in his right hand (representing the power of the Cross of Christ as a shield against evil) and his Rule in his left hand (signifying his spiritual teachings for monastic life).
- **Words around the edge:** Circling around Benedict are the Latin words: *"Eius in obitu nostro praesentia muniamur"* which translates to *"May we be strengthened by his presence in the hour of our*

death," reflecting the belief in Benedict's intercession at the time of death.

- **The Raven and the Poisoned Cup:** On the sides of Benedict are depictions of a raven and a poisoned cup. The cup, shattered by the sign of the cross, represents the first attempt on Benedict's life by poisoning, from which he was miraculously saved. The raven, who is seen carrying a poisoned loaf of bread, represents the second failed attempt on Benedict's life.

The **Back of the Medal:**

- **The Cross:** A large cross dominates the reverse side of the medal. The vertical and horizontal bars of the cross carry the initial letters of a rhythmic Latin prayer: *"Crux sacra sit mihi lux! Nunquam draco sit mihi dux!"* which translates as *"May the holy cross be my light! May the dragon never be my guide!"*
- **The Margins:** Around the margin of the back of the medal, the letters *V R S N S M V - S M Q L I V B* are the initial letters of the Latin prayer of exorcism against Satan (as previously noted): *"Vade retro Satana! Nunquam suade mihi vana! Sunt mala quae libas. Ipse venena bibas!"* In English, this translates to *"Begone Satan! Never tempt me with your vanities! What you offer me is evil. Drink the poison yourself!"*
- **Pax:** At the top of the medal is the word *"Pax"* *(Peace)*, the Benedictine motto, signaling the peace that comes from serving Christ.

It's important to note that the medal is not a "magical"

object or amulet, but rather a visible symbol and reminder of the truth of Benedict's life, his faith in God's protection, and his intercessory power. As with any other religious object, the graces associated with it come from God, and its power is derived from the faith and prayer of the user.

With that said, there must certainly be a reason why so many priests, including exorcists, consider the medal and its prayers to be such a powerful weapon against evil.

PART V

REGULA

Your way of acting should be different from the world's way;
the love of Christ must come first.

- Benedict

40

BENEDICT'S RULE

The Rule of St. Benedict is a foundational text for monastic life in the Christian West. It sets forth an outline for Christian discipleship that balances spiritual and manual work. Throughout its seventy-three chapters, the Rule covers a range of topics, including the qualities of an abbot, the care of the sick, guests, and the poor, and guidance on daily worship and work.

At the core of Benedict's Rule are three vows: stability (commitment to a particular community), conversion (life-long fidelity to monastic life and growth), and obedience (humble listening and conforming to the community's shared pursuit of holiness).

One of the most famous chapters is Chapter 4, "The Tools for Good Works," which is essentially a practical guide on how to love God and neighbor. It includes injunctions such as: *"Honor all men. Love the brotherhood. Fear God. Love not much talking."*

The Rule underscores the importance of balance in monastic life, encapsulated in the Latin phrase "Ora et

Labora" (Pray and Work). The daily schedule of a Benedictine monastery was split between prayer (both communal and private), reading (spiritual and secular), and manual labor.

"Idleness is the enemy of the soul. Therefore, the brothers should have specified periods for manual labor as well as for prayerful reading." (Chapter 48)

Humility is another central theme in the Rule. In Chapter 7, Benedict describes twelve steps of humility, which he sees as a ladder leading to heaven. The steps range from fearing God and giving up one's will to accepting hardships and confessing one's sins.

"Do not aspire to be called holy before you really are, but first be holy that you may more truly be called so." (Chapter 4)

Benedict's Rule also emphasizes the importance of listening, starting from the Prologue itself: *"Listen carefully, my son, to the master's instructions, and attend to them with the ear of your heart."* This famous opening sentence is a call to attentive and wholehearted listening, a prerequisite for spiritual growth and transformation.

The Rule provides guidance for living together as a community. It highlights the importance of mutual respect, kindness, and patience: *"Above all, do not neglect to be hospitable to one another in the community." (Chapter 53)*

While the Rule was initially written for monks, its wisdom extends to all Christians. Its timeless principles of balance, humility, and attentive listening provide a framework for a life devoted to seeking God, encouraging us to transform our daily tasks and challenges into opportunities for spiritual growth. The Rule of St. Benedict remains a significant source of spiritual guidance, even after 15 centuries of its inception.

41

TOOLS FOR GOOD WORKS

Chapter 4 of The Rule of St. Benedict, titled *"The Tools for Good Works,"* is a critical part of the spiritual guidebook provided by Benedict for monastics. This chapter details a comprehensive list of virtues and commandments that Benedict believed necessary for those in pursuit of a holy life, aligned to the ideals of monasticism. The chapter serves as a moral and ethical compass, providing practical guidance on how to live a life pleasing to God.

The chapter begins with the fundamental commandment: *"First of all, love the Lord God with your whole heart, your whole soul and all your strength, and love your neighbor as yourself,"* aligning with the two great commandments provided by Christ in the Gospels.

Benedict then enumerates 72 specific moral precepts. These precepts encompass many aspects of moral living, including love, respect, humility, and patience. Here are a few examples:

1. **Honor all men.**

2. Do not do to another what you do not want done to yourself.

3. Deny oneself in order to follow Christ.

4. Restrain the tongue and keep silence unless it is necessary to speak.

5. Daily in one's prayers, with tears and sighs, confess past sins to God, and amend them for the future.

6. Do not hate any man.

7. Do not be jealous or harbor envy.

8. Do not love strife.

9. Do not exercise vengeance.

The precepts are not only prohibitions of negative actions but also enjoin positive actions, encouraging things like hospitality, respect for the elderly, love for the young, and the pursuit of peace.

These prescriptions aim to cultivate a culture of love, peace, and mutual respect within the monastic community and the individual's relationship with God. They were intended to provide a practical and daily roadmap for monks to follow—aiding their journey towards spiritual growth and union with God—but can be applied to some degree in anyone's daily life.

42

12 STEPS OF HUMILITY

The twelve steps of humility, as laid out by Benedict in The Rule, constitute a spiritual ladder towards achieving true humility, which Benedict considered essential for anyone striving to attain the perfection of monastic life. The twelve steps are as follows:

1. **Fear of God:** Acknowledge that God is always watching and adjust your actions accordingly.
2. **Denial of Self-will:** Do not follow your own desires or passions but submit to the will of God.
3. **Obedience:** Follow the teachings of the Lord and obey your superiors in all things for the love of God.
4. **Patient Endurance:** Endure all hardships for the sake of God, believing that these trials lead to greater spiritual rewards.
5. **Confession of Sins:** Acknowledge your faults and imperfections, hiding nothing from God and your spiritual superiors.

6. **Acceptance of Lowliness:** Accept being considered inferior, worthless, and unimportant for the love of God.

7. **Belief in Inferiority:** Believe from the heart that you are indeed inferior and worthless.

8. **Following the Rules:** Follow the common rule of the monastery and the example set by your superiors.

9. **Silence:** Only speak when necessary, remembering the Scripture's caution that *"In the multitude of words, there shall not want sin" (Proverbs 10:19).*

10. **Restraint of Laughter:** Refrain from quick and easy laughter, for it is written: *"The fool lifts up his voice in laughter" (Ecclesiastes 21:23).*

11. **Few Words, Calm Speech:** Speak gently, humbly, and seriously, with few words and reasonable volume, especially in the presence of your superiors and elders.

12. **Humility in Behavior:** Show your humility in all your actions and appearances, remembering always your sinfulness and the punishment due to sin.

It's essential to understand that these steps were written for monks within a monastic setting, under the direction of a wise and balanced abbot. The steps are meant to foster a spirit of humility and obedience to aid in the pursuit of holiness. The full value and application of these steps might vary in different contexts, particularly in the modern world, but the core principles still hold universal spiritual value.

43

THE MASTER'S RULE

G iven Benedict's emphasis on humility and community, it's of little doubt that he would want some of the major influences on his life and writings to be mentioned.

One of these is The Rule of the Master, also referred to as The Master's Rule, a monastic rule written in the early sixth century, a document of profound influence on the development of Western monasticism.

Although The Rule of the Master was written anonymously and the authorship is still uncertain, its depth and detail seem to have significantly shaped the formulation of Benedict's Rule. Many scholars believe it was one of the sources from which Benedict drew inspiration in his own writings.

The Rule of the Master, known in Latin as "Regula Magistri," offers a detailed guideline for monastic life, covering a wide range of topics from daily routines, liturgical practices, spiritual readings, to the discipline of community members. Its emphasis on balance, moderation, and the spiritual growth of the individual monk resonated with Benedict, who sought to establish a monastic rule that was both practical and spiritually fulfilling.

Benedict, in devising his Rule, appears to have expanded on segments found in the Rule of the Master, though Benedict also includes new additions and modifications to suit his vision for monastic life.

For instance, both rules lay out a similar daily rhythm of prayer, work, and reading, following the dictum "Ora et Labora" (Pray and Work). However, Benedict's Rule is typically more tempered, avoiding the somewhat extreme ascetical practices found in the Rule of the Master.

Furthermore, Benedict seems to have adapted the Rule of the Master's teachings on humility, obedience, and community life. Benedict's famous chapter on humility (Chapter 7 of his Rule), although distinct in its arrangement and style, reflects similar passages in the Master's Rule.

Another difference lies in the language and tone. While the Rule of the Master tends to be verbose and at times harsh, Benedict's Rule is marked by its brevity, clarity, and compassion, famously advising abbots to "temper all things" so that monks "do not run away from the monastery, but stay and are saved."

The Rule of St. Benedict became one of the most influential guides for monastic life in the West, primarily due to its balance and practicality, and its capacity to adapt to varying circumstances. This adaptability is likely due in part to the influence of the Rule of the Master, which provided a comprehensive, if somewhat rigid, framework from which Benedict could draw.

While the Rule of the Master may not have achieved the widespread acceptance that Benedict's Rule did, its influence on the latter assures it a pivotal place in the history of Western monasticism. Benedict was able to draw from the raw material of the Master's Rule and shape it into a timeless guide for monastic life, a testament to the transformative power of discerning interpretation and wise application.

44

JOHN CASSIAN

John Cassian (circa 360-435 AD), a Christian monk and theologian celebrated for his writings on monastic life, deeply influenced a man who was yet to be born during his lifetime, a man who would later shape Western monasticism: St. Benedict of Nursia.

Cassian, like Benedict, was the son of wealthy parents and educated in the traditional Roman manner. And, in another similarity, Cassian turned his back on a worldly life to follow the path of monasticism.

His travels led him to the deserts of Egypt, where he spent a decade learning from the desert fathers. These experiences profoundly shaped his spiritual outlook, and he later penned two significant works: the "Institutes," detailing monastic practices and the eight principal vices, and the "Conferences," which profiled the wisdom of the desert fathers.

Around forty years after Cassian's death, Benedict was born into a noble family in Nursia, Italy. Just like Cassian, he left the comforts of his family's wealth and prestige to seek a life of holiness and devotion to God. Benedict's search for spiritual enlightenment eventually led him to write his own monastic rule known as the "Rule of St. Benedict," a guide for monastic life that balances prayer, work, and community living.

While direct references to Cassian in Benedict's Rule are not frequent, it is evident that Benedict had great respect for Cassian's wisdom. He mentions Cassian by name in Chapter 73, where he advises his monks to read *"the Conferences of the Fathers, their Institutes and their Lives, and also the Rule of our Holy Father Basil."*

Furthermore, a detailed analysis of the Rule reveals an implicit yet profound influence of Cassian's thinking. Cassian's stress on the importance of stability, the communal life of a monastery as opposed to the solitary life of a hermit, his approach to monastic obedience, and the importance of balancing work and prayer, all find echoes in Benedict's Rule.

Take, for example, Cassian's insights on dealing with the eight principal vices, particularly acedia or spiritual sloth. Cassian's detailed description of this spiritual affliction and its remedies has a clear influence on Benedict's Rule, which gives directions for the daily schedule of a monk—prayer, work, and rest—aimed at preventing idleness, which he regarded as the enemy of the soul.

Benedict's concept of a monastic leader as a spiritual father, responsible for the souls of his monks, bears striking similarities with the abbot's role described in Cassian's works. Both spiritual fathers agreed that an abbot should be wise, compassionate, discerning, and moderate, always considering the needs and capacities of his monks.

In conclusion, while they were separated by time and geography, St. Benedict of Nursia and John Cassian are intrinsically linked by a shared vision of monastic life. Benedict's Rule, which has shaped Western monasticism for over fifteen centuries, may not have been so powerful if not for the foundation laid by John Cassian's insights and wisdom.

45

BENEDICT'S HEROES

W hile exploring the people, circumstances, and experiences that shaped Benedict's vocation, it's equally important to understand the spiritual influences on Benedict himself. The saints to whom Benedict devoted his prayers and reverence are an illuminating lens to understand his spiritual inclinations.

St. John the Baptist

John the Baptist had a significant place in the devotional life of Benedict. This is illustrated by the dedication of the first church at Monte Cassino in his honor. The decision to dedicate this church to St. John the Baptist may have been influenced by the Church's liturgical calendar. During the time of the building's completion, the Feast of St. John the Baptist, celebrated on June 24, would have been a significant celebration.

The Apostles

Benedict showed great reverence towards the apostles. This is seen in the Rule of St. Benedict, where he included quotes and teachings from the apostles. For example, he used St. Peter's advice from his First Letter in the New

Testament, reminding the monks to *"cast all your anxieties on him, for he cares about you" (1 Peter 5:7).*

Furthermore, he dedicated the second church at Monte Cassino to St. Peter and St. Paul, indicating his great devotion to the pillars of the early Christian Church.

St. Martin of Tours

St. Martin of Tours was another saint greatly revered by Benedict. Known for his holiness and miraculous deeds, St. Martin was a model for monastic life in the West, and his influence is reflected in Benedict's writings. In the Rule, Benedict mentions St. Martin when discussing the care for the sick, emphasizing the importance of serving them as if serving Christ Himself, just as St. Martin did.

By observing those who influenced this foundational figure of Christian monasticism, we can gain deeper insights into the formation of his spirituality and, by extension, the Rule that continues to guide many religious communities to this day. Benedict's devotion reminds us that the communion of saints is a tapestry of spiritual guidance and mutual intercession, guiding us all towards a deeper relationship with God.

46

INSIDE A MONASTERY

Benedict's Rule sets out a detailed daily schedule for life in a Benedictine monastery. The rhythm of the day is organized around the Liturgy of the Hours, which is the cornerstone of monastic prayer, and it also includes periods for manual labor, reading, and meals. This balance of prayer, work, and study is a key feature of Benedictine life.

Here is a rough idea of how a typical day might look:

Vigils or Night Office (around 2:00-3:00 am): The first prayer of the day, this office includes several Psalms, a scripture reading, and other prayers.

Lauds or Morning Prayer (around dawn, often 6:00 am): This prayer includes Psalms of praise, a short scripture reading, and prayers to start the day.

Prime (around 7:00 am): A shorter office, marking the start of the working day.

Terce (around 9:00 am): The "third hour" prayer, after which the monks would traditionally go to manual labor.

Sext (around 12:00 pm): The "sixth hour" prayer, followed by the main meal of the day.

None (around 3:00 pm): The "ninth hour" prayer, followed by more work or study.

Vespers (in the evening, often around 6:00 pm): The "evening prayer", which includes Psalms, readings, and prayers, and is often considered the most important prayer after Lauds.

Compline (before bed, often around 7:30 pm): The "completion" prayer, a short, reflective office before bedtime.

The Great Silence: After Compline, a period of silence is observed throughout the night until the morning office of Lauds.

Between these periods of liturgical prayer, monks engage in manual labor, which might include tasks like gardening, cleaning, cooking, and maintenance around the monastery.

There is also time set aside for Lectio Divina, a form of prayerful reading of scripture and other spiritual texts. Meals are taken in silence while a book is being read aloud, and there's also time for rest and recreation.

It's important to note that the actual schedule can vary greatly between monasteries and even within the same monastery across different times of the year. However, the guiding principle remains the same: a balance of prayer, work, and study, underpinned by a commitment to communal living and the seeking of God in all things.

47

A MAN OF SANCTITY

odern-day understanding of the physical appearance and character of Benedict comes largely from artwork created after his death and the accounts written by Pope St. Gregory the Great in his work, the "Dialogues." However, as is often the case with saints from the early centuries of Christianity, explicit details about his physical features, dietary habits, or personal style are sparse.

From the "Dialogues," we gather that Benedict was a man of exceptional spiritual and moral character. Gregory writes, *"For the saintly man could not otherwise teach than he himself lived."* This quote points to Benedict's integrity, where his life and his teachings were one and the same.

Benedict was known for his deep prayer life and strong discipline. He was a man of silence, as is the monastic tradition, and he valued contemplation. He was also recognized for his gift of prophecy and spiritual insight, which he used to guide his monks and others who sought his advice.

As for his physical appearance and personal habits, we don't have specific details. However, considering the monastic lifestyle he led and propagated, we can infer certain things:

1. **Dress:** As a monk and abbot, Benedict would have worn a habit, the religious clothing of monks. The traditional Benedictine habit is black, signifying the death of the wearer to the world, and includes a tunic, a belt, a scapular, and a hood. Benedict's own Rule prescribes modest and simple clothing for monks, appropriate to the climate and work, without any extravagance.

2. **Food and Drink:** The Rule of St. Benedict prescribed a simple diet for his monks. They were typically to have two meals a day with a sufficient quantity of bread and a choice of cooked food. The Rule also allowed for a moderate amount of wine. It's reasonable to assume that Benedict himself followed a similar dietary regimen, characterized by moderation and simplicity.

3. **Personality:** St. Gregory the Great's "Dialogues" portray Benedict as a deeply humble, wise, and compassionate man. He was firm but fair in the leadership of his monks, balancing discipline with understanding. He had a heart for hospitality, as reflected in his Rule: *"Let all guests who arrive be received like Christ."*

Despite the lack of concrete eyewitness descriptions of Benedict's physical appearance or personal style, his character shines through the narratives and the legacy he left behind - that of a disciplined yet compassionate spiritual father, a guide, and a beacon of sanctity.

48

MEDITATIONS ON THE RULE

These quotes from the Rule of St. Benedict encapsulate his teachings on various aspects of monastic life, emphasizing the pursuit of God's love, community living, humility, hospitality, and the transformative power of spiritual discipline. They continue to inspire and guide individuals seeking a deeper commitment to a life of faith and service.

⁓

"LISTEN CAREFULLY, *my child, to your master's precepts, and incline the ear of your heart." (Prologue)*
This opening line emphasizes the importance of attentive listening and openness to the teachings and guidance of the spiritual leader.

⁓

"PREFER *nothing to the love of Christ." (Ch. 4)*
Benedict underscores the primacy of the love of Christ

above all other desires and attachments, urging monks to prioritize their devotion to God.

~

"IDLENESS IS the enemy of the soul." (Ch. 48)
Benedict recognizes the danger of idleness and encourages monks to engage in purposeful and productive activities that foster spiritual growth.

~

"PEACE IS NOT SIMPLY the absence of war." (Ch. 72)
Benedict challenges the notion of peace as mere absence of conflict, highlighting the need for active and intentional efforts to cultivate harmony, reconciliation, and unity.

~

"SO LET all be received as Christ Himself." (Ch. 61)
Benedict emphasizes the importance of treating all individuals, especially the weak and marginalized, with respect, dignity, and compassion, seeing the presence of Christ in them.

~

"RUN while you have the light of life." (Ch. 64)
Benedict encourages monks to seize the opportunity for spiritual growth and conversion, reminding them of the transient nature of life and the urgency to pursue holiness.

~

"YOUR WAY of acting should be different from the world's way." *(Ch. 4)*

Benedict calls monks to embrace a countercultural approach to life, challenging them to live according to the Gospel values rather than conforming to the worldly standards.

~

"YOUR PRAYER SHOULD BE SHORT, but full of heartfelt devotion." *(Ch. 20)*

Benedict encourages monks to cultivate a sincere and focused prayer life, emphasizing the importance of genuine devotion over the length of prayers.

~

"DO NOT BE TOO quick to accept or too stubborn to reject." *(Ch. 3)*

Benedict advises monks to exercise discernment and balance in their decision-making processes, urging them to be open to guidance while also exercising critical thinking.

~

"LET us do what the Prophet says: 'I said, I will guard my ways, that I may not sin with my tongue.'" *(Ch. 6)*

Benedict emphasizes the importance of cultivating self-control and guarding one's speech to avoid sinful or harmful words.

~

"THE LIFE of a monk ought to be a continuous Lent." *(Ch. 49)*

Benedict encourages a spirit of ongoing self-discipline and penitence, calling monks to live in a manner consistent with the penitential season of Lent.

～

"NEVER GIVE *a hollow greeting of peace or turn away when someone needs your love." (Ch. 4)*
Benedict emphasizes the importance of genuine compassion and active love, urging monks to extend care and support to others in need.

～

"LET *your good deeds be shown not by words but by deeds." (Ch. 4)*
Benedict reminds monks that their actions should align with their words, emphasizing the significance of living a life of integrity and authenticity.

～

"THEY SHOULD *each try to be the first to show respect to the other, supporting with the greatest patience one another's weaknesses of body or behavior, and earnestly competing in obedience to one another." (Ch. 72)*
Benedict emphasizes the virtues of humility, patience, and mutual support within the monastic community.

～

"WHENEVER YOU BEGIN *any good work, pray to God most earnestly to bring it to perfection." (Ch. 4)*
Benedict encourages monks to seek God's guidance and

assistance in all their endeavors, recognizing the necessity of divine grace for successful completion.

~

"LET the brethren ever bear in mind that at the Last Judgment of God there will be an examination of these and all other deeds of evil thoughts as well." (Ch. 7)
Benedict emphasizes the importance of accountability and the awareness that all actions will ultimately be subject to divine judgment.

~

"LET them prefer nothing whatever to Christ, and may he bring us all together to everlasting life." (Ch. 72)
Benedict reminds monks to keep Christ as their ultimate priority, seeking union with Him and anticipating the promise of eternal life.

~

"DO NOT BE DAUNTED IMMEDIATELY by fear and run away from the road that leads to salvation." (Ch. 7)
Benedict encourages perseverance in the face of challenges and setbacks, urging monks to remain steadfast on the path to salvation.

~

"THE ABBOT SHOULD ALWAYS REMEMBER what he is and remember what he is called, and he should know that to whom more is committed, from him more will be asked." (Ch. 2)
Benedict highlights the responsibilities of an abbot,

reminding them of their role as spiritual leaders and the accountability they bear.

~

"LET the young be shown a disciplined way of life with all moderation and seriousness." (Ch. 36)
Benedict emphasizes the importance of providing guidance and example to young members of the community, nurturing them in a balanced and disciplined manner.

~

"IN THE MONASTERY, let nothing be preferred to the work of God." (Ch. 43)
Benedict places the utmost importance on the communal prayer and worship, instructing monks to prioritize their participation in the Divine Office above all other tasks.

~

"DAY BY DAY, remind yourself that you are going to die." (Ch. 4)
Benedict encourages monks to contemplate the transitory nature of life and the urgency of living with a mindful awareness of their mortality.

~

"NEVER SWERVING FROM HIS INSTRUCTIONS, then, but faithfully observing his teaching in the monastery until death, we shall through patience share in the sufferings of Christ that we may deserve also to share in his kingdom." (Ch. 73)
Benedict emphasizes the lifelong commitment to faith-

fully follow his teachings, with the ultimate goal of sharing in the glory of Christ's kingdom.

~

"IN ALL THINGS, let all follow the Rule as guide." (Chapter 73)
Benedict emphasizes the Rule as the guiding principle for monastic life, ensuring order, discipline, and harmony within the community.

PART VI

LEGATUM

Let them prefer nothing whatever to Christ, and may he bring us all together to everlasting life.

- Benedict

49

BENEDICT'S INFLUENCE

Many saints and holy men and women throughout the centuries have admired and been influenced by Benedict and his teachings, particularly his "Rule". Here are a few instances where saints have indirectly referenced the influence of Benedict in their lives:

1. **St. Gregory the Great** wrote about Benedict extensively in his "Dialogues". One of his often-cited quotes is, *"The man of God, Benedict, being diligent in watching, rose early up before the time of matins (his monks being yet at rest) and came to the window of his chamber, where he offered up his prayers to almighty God."*

2. **St. John Paul II**, in his Apostolic Letter *"Pacis Nuntius,"* wrote: *"Europe owes to Benedict, in particular, that after the fall of the Roman Empire, it did not succumb to the barbarian invasions, but rediscovered the primacy of the spiritual dimension in human life."* While not a contemporary of

Benedict, St. John Paul II acknowledges the foundational role that Benedict played in shaping Western monasticism and, indeed, European culture.

3. **St. Thérèse of Lisieux** had a profound respect for the Benedictine spirituality. In a letter to her sister Céline, she wrote: *"Our holy Father Benedict is really and truly our Father, just like our glorious patriarch St. John of the Cross... I find that the Benedictine and Carmelite vocation are the same, they both have the same goal: union with God."*

Many other saints have lived by his Rule and were undoubtedly influenced by his teachings. The monastic life, as shaped by Benedict, had an extensive impact on numerous religious orders and communities that came after him. The Benedictine Order has made significant contributions to the Church over its long history, including numerous saints and popes. Here are a few notable examples:

1. **St. Scholastica (c. 480 – 543):** St. Scholastica was the twin sister of Benedict and the foundress of the female branch of Benedictine Monasticism. She is the patron saint of nuns and is invoked against storms and rain.

2. **St. Bede the Venerable (c. 673-735):** An English Benedictine monk at the monastery of St. Peter and its companion monastery of St. Paul in the Kingdom of Northumbria. He's well known as an author and scholar, and his most famous work, "Historia ecclesiastica gentis Anglorum" (The Ecclesiastical History of the English

People) gained him the title "The Father of English History".

3. **St. Hildegard of Bingen (1098-1179):** A German Benedictine abbess, she was known for her wide range of contributions to theology, botany, and medicine, and she composed music and wrote about natural history and medicinal uses for various plants and animals. She is recognized as a Doctor of the Church.

4. **St. Gertrude the Great (1256 – c. 1302):** She was a German Benedictine nun, mystic, and theologian. She is the only woman saint to be called "the Great". Her most famous work is "The Herald of Divine Love," and she had a profound devotion to the Sacred Heart of Jesus, long before the popularization of this devotion.

5. **St. Francis of Assisi** didn't leave any quotes specifically about Benedict, but he visited Subiaco, a place closely linked to Benedict. In fact, Nursia is located only 28 miles from Assisi, and both are part of the same Italian region, Umbria. Subiaco, near Rome, is only about 80 miles from Assisi. The fresco in the Sacro Speco, depicting St. Francis with the stigmata, is a silent testimony of the meeting of two spiritualities.

6. **St. Bernard of Clairvaux,** a Cistercian monk whose order followed the Rule of St. Benedict, said, *"The Benedictine monk ought to be a man of the Gospel, 'following the Lamb wherever he goes.'"*

7. **St. Hildegard of Bingen,** a German Benedictine abbess, she was known for her wide range of contributions to theology, botany, and medicine, and she composed music and wrote about

natural history and medicinal uses for various plants and animals. She is recognized as a Doctor of the Church and demonstrated the Benedictine influence in her life through her works. While there are no direct quotes, her belief that *"All the arts come from God and are to be respected as divine gifts"* echoes the balanced approach to work and prayer in the Benedictine tradition.

Each of these Benedictines, in their roles as saints and popes, significantly influenced the Catholic Church and helped to shape its history.

50

SACRED SITES

Benedict, as one of the most influential saints in the Christian tradition, has numerous sacred sites associated with his life and works. These sites have become important places of pilgrimage for people seeking spiritual inspiration, healing, or a deeper understanding of the monastic tradition. Here are some of the most notable:

1. **The Abbey of Monte Cassino (Italy):** This is the location where Benedict founded his monastic community and wrote the Rule. The abbey was destroyed and rebuilt several times throughout history, with the most recent reconstruction after World War II. Today, it serves as a place of pilgrimage and contains relics of Benedict and his sister, St. Scholastica.

2. **Subiaco Monastery (Italy):** Before moving to Monte Cassino, Benedict spent about three years in solitary prayer in a cave at Subiaco. A monastery was later built around this cave, known as the "Sacro Speco" (Holy Cave). The

frescoes in the monastery, some of which date
back to the 13th century, depict scenes from the
lives of Christ and Benedict.

3. **The Basilica of Benedict in Norcia (Italy):** The
basilica stands on the site where it's believed
Benedict and his twin sister, St. Scholastica,
were born. The original basilica was severely
damaged in an earthquake in 2016 but has since
been rebuilt.

4. **Benedict's Abbey, Atchison, Kansas (USA):** One
of the most prominent Benedictine monasteries
in the United States, this abbey is a vibrant
center for prayer and study.

5. **Einsiedeln Abbey (Switzerland):** This is one of
the most significant Benedictine monasteries in
Europe. Its Black Madonna has attracted
pilgrims since the Middle Ages.

6. **Benedict Chapel, Sumvitg, Switzerland:**
Designed by the renowned Swiss architect Peter
Zumthor, this modern chapel is dedicated to
Benedict. Its minimalist design serves to focus
attention on the liturgy.

7. **Buckfast Abbey (England):** This abbey in
Devon has been home to Benedictine monks for
over a thousand years. The monks are known
for their Buckfast Tonic Wine, a recipe
developed in the abbey in the 19th century.

8. **The Abbey of St. Benoit du Lac (Canada):**
Founded in 1912 by Benedictine monks from
France, this abbey in Quebec is known for its
Gregorian chants and apple cider.

9. **Monastery of St. Benet de Montserrat (Spain):**
This monastery located near Barcelona is a

pilgrimage site with a statue of the Virgin Mary and an active Benedictine community.

10. **The Abbey of Saint-Germain-des-Prés, Paris (France):** Though no longer an active monastery, this site is notable as the oldest church in Paris. It was initially established by Childebert I to house the relics of St. Vincent, and later reformed by Benedictines.

Each of these sites, in their own unique ways, continues to uphold and spread the Benedictine tradition of "ora et labora" - prayer and work. Whether through ancient art, beautiful Gregorian chant, or the quiet demonstration of monastic life, these locations inspire visitors to seek a deeper spiritual connection.

51

A SAINT BEFORE SAINTS

Having passed away in 547 AD, Benedict lived in an era before the formal canonization process was standardized by the Roman Catholic Church. His recognition as a saint was based on his reputation for holiness, miracles attributed to him, and the widespread veneration among the faithful.

The veneration of Benedict began soon after his death and was perpetuated by the monastic communities he founded. The monasteries served not only as living memorials to his holy life but also as centers for the propagation of his teachings and the Rule he wrote for monastic life.

Benedict's life, miracles, and teachings were also widely publicized by Pope St. Gregory the Great in his "Dialogues," written around 593-594 AD. This influential work, which included a biography of Benedict, helped spread the veneration of Benedict throughout the Christian world.

By the late Middle Ages, Benedict was honored as a patron saint of Europe, reflecting his significant influence on European monasticism and Christian culture. Over

time, numerous miracles were attributed to his intercession, further solidifying his reputation as a saint.

The formal canonization process as we understand it
today – involving thorough investigation of a candidate's
life, writings, miracles, and a formal declaration by the
Pope – was not established until the 10th century and was
not standardized until the 12th century, long after Benedict's time.

However, his profound impact on monasticism, his
exemplary life of prayer and work, and the numerous miracles associated with him, made his recognition as a saint a
natural development within the Christian tradition. Even
without a formal canonization process, Benedict is venerated as a significant figure in the Church's history.

In fact, Pope Paul VI proclaimed Benedict the patron
protector of Europe due to his crucial role in the Christian-
ization and the rise of civilization in the continent after the
fall of the Roman Empire. Since then, Benedict has been
venerated as the **Patron Saint of Europe** as well as
numerous other causes and professions, including:

1. **Monks and Monastic Communities:** As the
   founder of western monasticism, he is the
   patron saint of monks and monastic
   communities worldwide.
2. **Students:** Given his influence on the tradition of
   monastic schools, Benedict is considered a
   patron saint of students.
3. **Farmers:** The Benedictine monastic order
   contributed significantly to the development of
   farming practices in the Middle Ages, making
   Benedict the patron of farmers.
4. **Cavers and Speleologists:** Because Benedict
   lived as a hermit in a cave for three years, he is

the patron saint of those who explore caves (speleologists) and cavers.

5. **Civil Engineers:** This patronage comes from the numerous construction projects he would have overseen at his monasteries.

6. **Kidney Disease:** He is invoked by those suffering from kidney disease. This could be due to an episode in his life when he was given a poisoned drink but miraculously survived.

7. **Poisoning:** After surviving attempts to poison him, he became the patron saint against poisoning.

8. **Gall stones:** Benedict is also invoked by those suffering from gall stones.

9. **Dying People:** He is also considered a patron of a happy death, as he died in prayer after receiving the Eucharist.

In addition to these, people often invoke Benedict's intercession for protection against evil, reflected in the well-known St. Benedict Medal.

Formerly observed on March 21, the day of his death, the feast of Benedict was moved to July 11 in the liturgical calendar by Pope Paul VI in 1969. The primary reason for this change was that March 21 often falls during Lent, a penitential season of the Church year leading up to Easter. As such, the full celebration of saints' feasts during this time can be overshadowed by the Lenten observance.

The date of July 11 was chosen because it is the anniversary of the translation or movement of Benedict's relics to the Church of St. Benoit-sur-Loire, France, a significant event in Benedictine history.

The shift to July 11 allows for a more festive celebration of Benedict's life and contributions, free from the penitential context of the Lenten season. It provides the faithful, and especially those in the Benedictine order, the opportunity to honor Benedict's legacy and to seek his intercession in a joyful manner.

Benedictine devotion, however, is a year-round, life-long practice for many Catholics, especially monastics and exorcists.

52

THE BENEDICTINE WAY

B enedict's legacy is truly remarkable and continues to influence the Church and Western civilization to this day. His most significant contribution was undoubtedly the "Rule of St. Benedict," which became the guiding document for monastic life in the Christian West.

His Rule, with its balance of prayer and work, hospitality, and communal living, was adopted by countless monastic communities throughout the Middle Ages. Benedictine monasteries became centers of learning, scholarship, and culture, preserving much of the classical knowledge that might have otherwise been lost during the so-called "Dark Ages." They were instrumental in the development of agriculture, the brewing of beer, and the production of manuscripts and books, thus playing a pivotal role in the shaping of European civilization.

Benedict was canonized by Pope Honorius III in the 13th century. In 1964, Pope Paul VI proclaimed him the patron saint of Europe, recognizing the immense influence he had on the continent's Christian and cultural heritage.

Devotion to Benedict has remained strong throughout

the centuries. The Medal of Benedict, one of the most recognized Christian sacramental symbols, dates back to at least the 17th century. The medal is rich in symbolism, with inscriptions that encapsulate the heart of Benedict's teaching, including the famous motto "Pax" (Peace) and "Crux Sacra Sit Mihi Lux" (May the Holy Cross Be My Light). It is often used in the Church as a means of protection and a tool of exorcism.

Benedictine spirituality continues to inspire and guide millions, even those outside monastic communities. The Rule's timeless wisdom transcends the cloister and speaks to the hearts of all seeking a more profound spiritual life. Modern movements such as the Lay Cistercians and the Benedictine Oblates allow laypeople to incorporate the wisdom of Benedict's Rule into their daily lives.

In recent years, the popularity of Benedict has surged amid a revived interest in contemplative spirituality and the monastic tradition's simplicity. His emphasis on balance, hospitality, and community resonates deeply with modern seekers yearning for authentic spiritual engagement.

Benedict's enduring legacy is a testament to the power of his humble obedience to God's call. In an age often characterized by noise and haste, the message of Benedict – his call to prayer, silence, work, and community – remains as relevant and needed as ever.

53

INCORRUPTIBLE

A testament to Benedict's sanctity came many centuries after his death, a sign from God that further underscored the enduring impact of his life and teachings. The year was 1592, over a thousand years since Benedict had left this earthly plane. In a series of events ordained by the Church, his resting place in the Abbey of Monte Cassino was disturbed, the holy grounds excavated to reveal the mortal remains of the beloved saint.

His grave, hallowed by the passage of centuries, lay undisturbed until that fateful day. With the blessings of the Church and in the presence of devout followers, the grave was reverently opened. As the stone lid was lifted, an astonishing sight met the eyes of the observers - the body of Benedict lay intact, seemingly untouched by the relentless march of time.

In an extraordinary manifestation of divine preservation, Benedict's body was found without the common signs of decay that nature invariably inflicts upon mortal remains. His physical form, much like his spiritual legacy, appeared to withstand the test of time, mirroring the enduring relevance of his teachings and his Rule.

Such incidents of incorruptibility are considered by the Catholic Church as miraculous signs of sanctity. They point to the person's holy life and God's favor upon them. For the faithful, the incorruptibility of Benedict's body served as a profound reminder of the saint's teachings on the imper-manence of life, the inevitability of death, and the eternal nature of the soul.

The news of this discovery spread far and wide, strengthening the faith of many and attracting new followers to the Benedictine Order.

Even in death, Benedict continued to be a beacon of hope and faith. His incorrupt body served as a testament to his saintly life, reinforcing his teachings about the tempo-rary nature of earthly existence and the eternal promise of life everlasting. Just as Benedict urged his followers to constantly remember their mortality, his incorruptibility pointed towards the divine promise of life beyond death.

After the discovery of Benedict's incorrupt body in 1592, his remains were reinterred at the Abbey of Monte Cassino with great reverence. They continue to be a point of venera-tion for the faithful, who make pilgrimages to the Abbey to pay their respects and seek Benedict's intercession.

It is important to note that in 1944, during World War II, the Abbey was severely damaged by bombing. While the restoration process was extensive and careful, it is believed that the precise identification of Benedict's remains was lost in the process.

However, according to tradition, the relics of both Bene-dict and his twin sister, St. Scholastica, are interred in the same sarcophagus, located under the high altar of the basilica at the Abbey of Monte Cassino. This place of burial continues to hold a deep spiritual significance for followers of Benedict's teachings and those devoted to his spiritual path. The sarcophagus and the abbey remain an enduring testament to the legacy of Benedict and his enduring influence on Christian monasticism and spirituality.

Nevertheless, it is not the physical remains of Benedict that captivate the faithful. Rather, it is his spiritual legacy—his Rule, his virtues, and his influence—that continue to inspire people from all walks of life to lead a life rooted in prayer, work, stability, and community. This is the real enduring presence of Benedict in the world.

PART VII

ORATIO

Let them yearn for everlasting life with holy desire. Day by day let them remember that they are going to die.

- Benedict

54

EXORCISM PRAYER

While these prayers can be used in general Catholic devotions, they are especially potent when invoking the intercession of Benedict, especially in situations of spiritual struggle or protection from harm.

The **Benedict Exorcism Prayer** is a powerful prayer seeking protection against the influence and attacks of evil. It is often used to invoke the intercession of Benedict in times of spiritual warfare.

Latin

"Crux sacra sit mihi lux
Non draco sit mihi dux
Vade retro, Satana!
Numquam suade mihi vana
Sunt mala quae libas
Ipse venena bibas!"

English

"The Holy Cross be my light,
Let not the dragon be my guide.

Step back, Satan!
Never tempt me with your vanities.
What you offer me is evil;
Drink the poison yourself!"

55

PRAYER FOR PROTECTION

O glorious Benedict,
       sublime model of all virtues,
       pure vessel of God's grace!

BEHOLD ME, *humbly kneeling at your feet.*
    I implore you, in your loving kindness,
    to pray for me before the throne of God.

TO YOU, *I have recourse in all the dangers*
    which daily surround me.

SHIELD ME AGAINST MY ENEMIES,
    inspire me to imitate you in all things.

MAY *your blessing be with me always,*

so that I may shun whatever God forbids
and avoid the occasions of sin.
Amen.

56

A HAPPY DEATH

O holy Father, Benedict,
blessed by God both in grace and in name,
who, while standing in prayer,
with hands raised to heaven,
didst most happily yield thy angelic spirit
into the hands of thy Creator,
and hast promised zealously to defend
against all the snares of the enemy
in the last struggle of death,
those who shall daily remind thee
of thy glorious departure and heavenly joys;
protect me, I beseech thee, O glorious Father,
this day and every day by thy holy blessing,
that I may never be separated from our Lord,
from the company of thyself and of all the blessed.
Through the same Christ our Lord.
Amen.

57

INTERCESSORY PRAYER

May the intercession of the
Blessed Patriarch and Abbot Benedict
render Thee merciful unto us, O Lord,
that what our own unworthiness cannot obtain,
we may receive through his powerful patronage.

THROUGH CHRIST our Lord who lives and reigns
with Thee and the Holy Ghost, now and forever.

AMEN.

58

BENEDICT BLESSING PRAYER

T his responsorial prayer is a special blessing that is intended to be performed by a priest in the presence of a Benedict cross or medal.

FOR LAY PEOPLE who wish to have their medals or crosses blessed, we encourage you to ask a local priest to perform the blessing on your religious articles.

V: *Our help is in the name of the Lord.*

R: *Who made heaven and earth.*

In the name of God the Father + almighty, who made heaven and earth, the seas and all that is in them, I exorcise this {medal or cross} against the power and attacks of the evil one.

May all who use these medals devoutly be blessed with health of soul and body.

In the name of the Father + almighty, of the Son + Jesus Christ our Lord, and of the Holy + Spirit the Paraclete, and in the love of the same Lord Jesus Christ who will come on the last day to judge the living and the dead.

59

LITANY OF BENEDICT

T his litany of Benedict is a series of invocations and prayers to honor and seek the intercession of Benedict.

Lord, have mercy on us.

Christ, have mercy on us.

Lord, have mercy on us.

Christ, hear us.

Christ, graciously hear us.

God the Father of Heaven, have mercy on us.

God the Son, Redeemer of the world, have mercy on us.

God the Holy Spirit, have mercy on us.

Holy Trinity, one God, have mercy on us.

Holy Mary, pray for us.

Holy Mother of God, pray for us.

Holy Virgin of virgins, pray for us.

Benedict, renowned for your sanctity, pray for us.

Benedict, inflamed with the love of God, pray for us.

Benedict, distinguished for your virtues, pray for us.

Benedict, humble and obedient servant, pray for us.

Benedict, example of silence and solitude, pray for us.

Benedict, model of prayer and contemplation, pray for us.

Benedict, image of serenity and peace, pray for us.

Benedict, devoted seeker of God, pray for us.

Benedict, faithful guardian of the Rule, pray for us.

Benedict, teacher of moderation and temperance, pray for us.

Benedict, steadfast in times of temptation, pray for us.

Benedict, conqueror of the Evil One, pray for us.

Benedict, protector against spiritual darkness, pray for us.

Benedict, source of strength in adversity, pray for us.

Benedict, patron of monks and nuns, pray for us.

Benedict, intercessor for those in need, pray for us.

Benedict, defender of the Catholic faith, pray for us.

Benedict, advocate for a holy death, pray for us.

Lamb of God, who takes away the sins of the world, spare us, O Lord.

Lamb of God, who takes away the sins of the world, graciously hear us, O Lord.

Lamb of God, who takes away the sins of the world, have mercy on us.

Let us pray: *O God, who granted Benedict the grace to serve You faithfully and become a shining light in the monastic tradition, grant that, through his intercession, we may be strengthened in our commitment to holiness and find protection from all spiritual dangers. Through Christ our Lord. Amen.*

60

NOVENA TO BENEDICT

This novena to Benedict is a devotional prayer and may be adapted or modified according to personal preference or local traditions.

Instructions:

1. Begin the novena on nine consecutive days, preferably starting on the feast day of Benedict (July 11th) or any other date of personal significance.
2. Find a quiet and comfortable place for prayer, free from distractions.
3. Begin each day of the novena with an opening prayer.
4. Read and meditate on the daily reflection or intention.
5. Recite the prayer to Benedict.
6. Conclude each day with the closing prayer.

Opening Prayer: *O glorious Benedict, blessed servant of*

God, you who embraced a life of humility, prayer, and obedience, we come before you seeking your intercession. Help us to follow your example and draw closer to God with a sincere and humble heart. Benedict, pray for us. Amen.

Day 1 Reflection/Intention: Pray for an increase in faith

Prayer to Benedict: *Glorious Benedict, you who trusted in God's providence and had unwavering faith, we humbly ask for your intercession. Help us to deepen our faith, to trust in God's plan for our lives, and to seek His will above all else. Benedict, pray for us. Amen.*

Closing Prayer: *Benedict, your life is an inspiration to all who seek God's guidance and grace. As we conclude this day of prayer, we ask for your continued intercession and protection. Help us to live according to God's commandments and to grow in holiness each day. Benedict, pray for us. Amen.*

Day 2 Reflection/Intention: Pray for an increase in humility

Prayer to Benedict: *Glorious Benedict, you who embraced a life of humility and self-denial, we humbly ask for your intercession. Help us to recognize our weaknesses, to practice humility in our thoughts, words, and actions, and to always acknowledge our dependence on God's grace. Benedict, pray for us. Amen.*

Closing Prayer: *Benedict, your humility and submission to God's will inspire us to follow in your footsteps. As we conclude this day of prayer, we ask for your continued intercession and guidance. Help us to grow in humility and to always seek the greater glory of God. Benedict, pray for us. Amen.*

Continue the pattern of reflection, prayer to Benedict, and closing prayer for the remaining seven days of the novena, each day focusing on a specific intention or theme such as obedience, purity, charity, or protection against evil.

Concluding Prayer (Day 9): *O glorious Benedict, your life* *of holiness and devotion to God serves as an example for us all. As we complete this novena, we thank you for your intercession and ask for your continued presence in our lives. Help us to live out the principles of your holy Rule, so that we may grow in virtue and strive for sanctity. Benedict, pray for us. Amen.*

61

TRADITIONAL NOVENA PRAYER

This age-old prayer to Benedict can be used in the Benedict novena.

Glorious Benedict, sublime model of virtue, pure vessel of God's grace! Behold me humbly kneeling at your feet.

I implore you in your loving kindness to pray for me before the throne Of God. To you I have recourse in the dangers that daily surround me.

Shield me against my selfishness and my indifference to God and to my neighbor. Inspire me to imitate you in all things.

May your blessing be with me always, so that I may see and serve Christ in others and work for His kingdom. Graciously obtain for me from God those favors and graces which I need so much in the trials, miseries and afflictions of life.

Your heart was always full of love, compassion and mercy toward those who were afflicted or troubled in any way. You never dismissed without consolation and assistance anyone who had recourse to you.

I therefore invoke your powerful intercession, confident in the hope that you will hear my prayer and obtain for me the special grace and favor I earnestly implore.

Help me, great Benedict. to live and die as a faithful child of God, to run in the sweetness of His loving will and to attain the eternal happiness of heaven.

Amen.

62

CHAPLET OF BENEDICT

This Chaplet of Benedict was created by
CatholicShop.com to honor Benedict's life, his
monastic rule, and his virtues, with a particular
focus on his role as a protector against evil and temptation.
The chaplet is designed for use with a traditional five-
decade rosary.

1. **Begin at the Crucifix:** Start by making the *Sign
   of the Cross* and then recite the *Apostles' Creed.*
2. **On the first large bead, pray the Lord's Prayer:**
   This is in honor of Benedict's devotion to prayer
   and the will of God.
3. **On the three small beads, pray three Hail
   Mary's:** Each *Hail Mary* represents a core value
   of Benedict's Rule: Ora (Prayer), Labora (Work),
   and Lectio (Reading).
4. **On the next large bead, recite the Glory Be:**
   This is in honor of Benedict's devotion to the
   glory of God.

5. **On the centerpiece,** pray: *"Benedict, guide us in the path of virtue, deliver us from evil and lead us to eternal salvation."*

6. **On each large bead of the five decades,** reflect on a particular moment in Benedict's life or a particular virtue he exemplified, and recite the Lord's Prayer.

7. **First Decade:** Benedict's Triumph over Temptation: Reflect on his strength and courage when he rolled in the thorny bush to conquer his temptation.

8. **Second Decade:** Benedict's Flight from Rome: Reflect on his willingness to forsake worldly goods and prestige in pursuit of spiritual fulfillment.

9. **Third Decade:** Benedict's Miracle of the Broken Sieve: Reflect on his humility and faith in the midst of miraculous occurrences.

10. **Fourth Decade:** The Rule of St. Benedict: Reflect on the wisdom and charity demonstrated in his rule.

11. **Fifth Decade:** Benedict's Victory over Evil: Reflect on his steadfastness in the face of evil and his role as a protector against it.

12. **On the ten small beads of each decade,** meditate on the chosen reflection and pray ten Hail Mary's.

13. **At the end of each decade,** pray the *Glory Be* and the *Fatima Prayer.*

14. **After the fifth decade,** conclude with the Hail Holy Queen and end with the Sign of the Cross.

15. **Lastly, recite the following prayer:** *"Benedict, we honor your life, your Rule, and your battle against evil. Through your intercession, may we stand*

strong in our faith, resist temptation, and remain
ever-mindful of God's presence in our lives. Amen."

This chaplet incorporates the spiritual journey and virtuous life of Benedict, making it a meaningful devotion for those seeking to invoke his intercession, particularly against evil and temptation.

63

TRADITIONAL INVOCATION

Holy Benedict, we honor you for your self-sacrifice and solitary devotion to our Lord. May your life of prayer and contemplation inspire in all of us a similar respect for holiness and deep spirituality. We thank you for the Rule of St. Benedict and the strength and example of your monastic commitment. All things begin when we listen to the voice of God. Amen.

BECOMING BENEDICTINE

I n a world that often clamors with noise and chaos, Benedict's teachings remind us of the value of silence, prayer, and reflection, offering a path to personal transformation and deeper communion with God.

Many who reflect upon St. Benedict of Nursia's remarkable life find themselves called to adopt his spirit of perseverance, humility, and dedication to prayer and work. His rule reminds us of the essential balance between the spiritual and the practical, urging us to incorporate both in our lives.

The Rule of St. Benedict, a cornerstone of Western monasticism, is not just a guide for monks, but also a rich source of wisdom that can be applied in our everyday lives – in families, friendships, and careers.

While most of us may not live in monasteries, the principles embedded in the Rule – such as mindfulness, respect, balance, and humility – are as relevant today as they were in the sixth century.

Here are some ways in which we can incorporate the spirit of Benedict into our daily lives:

1. **Mindfulness and Prayer:** Benedictine monks start and end their day with prayer, a practice reminding us of the importance of mindfulness. Setting aside regular moments for reflection, meditation, or prayer can provide a sense of peace and perspective, helping us navigate the challenges of life.

2. **Balance:** "Ora et Labora" - prayer and work - is at the heart of the Benedictine Rule. This principle reminds us of the importance of a balanced life. While work and career are essential, so too is our spiritual, physical, and mental well-being. Prioritize time for relaxation, hobbies, and connecting with others, along with work commitments.

3. **Respect for All:** Benedict's Rule emphasizes treating every person with respect and dignity, as if you were welcoming Christ himself. This approach, when applied to our interactions with family, friends, and colleagues, fosters stronger relationships and better collaboration.

4. **Community and Hospitality:** The Rule encourages living in community and offering hospitality. In our context, this can be interpreted as building strong support networks and being there for others in times of need. In the workplace, fostering a sense of community can improve morale and productivity.

5. **Listening and Humility:** The Rule starts with the word "Listen" and often refers to humility. Actively listening to others and acknowledging that we do not have all the answers can enhance our understanding, resolve conflicts, and foster deeper connections. It also aids in personal

growth and better decision-making in our careers.

6. **Stewardship:** The Benedictine vow of stability can translate into a commitment to care for our immediate environment - home, workplace, and the earth. By treating all resources as sacred gifts, we can develop a sense of responsibility and respect towards them, leading to sustainable and ethical living.

7. **Continuous Growth:** The concept of 'conversatio morum' in the Rule suggests an ongoing commitment to spiritual and moral improvement. In modern terms, this underlines the value of lifelong learning and personal development.

In essence, The Rule of St. Benedict offers us a roadmap to a more fulfilling life. By integrating these age-old principles into our modern existence, we can cultivate a more balanced, respectful, and thoughtful approach to our lives, families, friendships, and careers. The wisdom of the Rule is indeed timeless, providing guidance and solace even in our fast-paced, modern world.

Benedict's legacy, both in the shape of Western monasticism and in the spiritual insights he bequeathed, continues to resonate powerfully with Catholics worldwide. As Benedict himself once wrote, *"Listen carefully, my son, to the master's instructions, and attend to them with the ear of your heart."*

May we all strive to listen more deeply and love more fully, in the spirit of this great saint.

Finis

CATHOLIC SHOP

Shop for **St. Benedict medals**, rosaries,
crucifixes, bracelets, and more
at *CatholicShop.com*

CRUX SACRA

CRUX SACRA
SIT MIHI
LUX

MAY THE
HOLY CROSS
BE MY LIGHT

PRAYER INVOCATIONS ON
THE ST. BENEDICT MEDAL

**Crux sancti patris
Benedicti (CSPB)**
*The Cross of Holy
Father Benedict*

**Eius in obitu nostro
praesentia muniamur!**
*May we be strengthened by his
presence in the hour of our death.*

**Crux sacra sit mihi lux!
Non draco sit mihi dux!**
*May the holy cross be my light!
May the dragon never be my guide!*

**Vade retro Satana! Nunquam
suade mihi vana! (V R S N S M V)**
*Begone Satan! Never tempt me
with your vanities!*

**Sunt mala quae libas. Ipse
venena bibas! (S M Q L I V B)**
*What you offer me is evil.
Drink the poison yourself!*